Dogs and
Their People

Dogs and Their People

Choosing and Training the Best Dog for You

Steve Diller

HYPERION
New York

Library of Congress Cataloging-in-Publication Data

Diller, Steve.

    Dogs and their people : choosing and training the best dog for you / Steve Diller.
    —1st ed.
      p. cm.
    ISBN 0-7868-6361-7
    1. Dogs. 2. Dogs—Selection. 3. Dog breeds. 4. Dogs—Training. 5. Dogs—Behavior.
    I. Title.
    SF426.D55 1998   98-7014
    636.7'088'7—dc21   CIP

First Edition

10 9 8 7 6 5 4 3 2 1

Contents

Introduction

People often ask me how I got into dogs. The answer is I did not get into them, they were a part of me. Perhaps there is an inherent component to my addiction. I have had the great pleasure of living with dogs all my life. In school every report I ever had to write was on the subject of dogs. My topics included the different breeds, the incredible variations of their body types as well as their intended functions as man's best friend. For me, loving dogs was as natural as breathing.

Dogs are a source of constant learning for me. The entire subject of dogs is a picture to be studied and improved upon over a lifetime. The emotional pulses of my dog experiences are infinite, unfortunately words are a poor vehicle to describe them to you. As puppies, dogs have taught me how to cope with life, and as my friends grew old they taught me to cope with death. For this I am grateful.

The field of veterinary technology turned my innate love of animals into a scientific quest for knowledge. I became fascinated with the medical field and enrolled in a clinical laboratory technology program. I learned hematology, how to analyze blood chemistry, urine samples, and serology (bloody typing). I learned radiology, parasitology, anesthesiology, and surgical nursing on the job. My ability to read and handle animals simply stems from the sheer number of pets I've encountered over the course of so many years. The veterinary specialists that I have had the benefit of working with over the years played an instrumental part in my overall education. Veterinary dermatologists, ophthalmologists, internists, surgeons, and neurologists taught me the wonders of veterinary medicine.

I was also exposed to the canine paraprofessions while working in animal hospitals. Dog groomers seemed to be increasing in magical numbers over the years, while I learned what a good haircut looks like. The dog grooming business is a tough one because a good haircut is one that the dog owner is happy with, even though it may not be correct for the breed. On the other hand, I have watched owners almost pass out from holding their breath when they saw their dog shaved down to the skin due to impossible hair matting. I read a sign in a dog grooming shop once that read "God does not cut hair and I do not do miracles." Miracles are, in my opinion, what people expect from dog professionals. Veterinarians are expected to bring health to terminal patients, groomers are expected to turn mops into models, and dog trainers are supposed to turn Cujo into Rin Tin Tin. I had to learn how to positively affect the mind-set of pet owners and teach them how to develop realistic goals for their pet's health and behavior. The combination of the right choice of dog and an attainable goal makes for a successful relationship. Let us move on to how to find that dog.

Dogs and Their People

1.

Should I Be a Dog Owner?

The Big Picture

I am often faced with telephone calls from potential new dog owners asking for help on which breeds might be appropriate for their lifestyle. Before I counsel a family on which breed might be best, I find it helpful to have the family first look at the basic issues governing the ultimate decision. To see the big picture, attempt to visualize what requirements are needed for successful dog ownership. In order for you to become a happy dog owner you should carefully examine your motives for wanting a dog and only then come to a logical breed choice, given a select group of criteria.

The deciding factor that determines whether or not a dog will live its entire life happily with your family rests upon making the right decision. You should ask yourself many questions. Should I be a dog owner? Do I understand all of the components to successful dog own-ership? Can I fulfill the needs of the new dog? What are the needs of the dog anyway? What are my needs?

You will need to be honest with yourself to find the right pooch and understand that your lifestyle will help to dictate your specific breed parameters.

Can you satisfy the primary needs of your dog? These responsi-bilities will include provisions for housing, adequate nutrition, and medical care. If you obtain a dog with a long coat, you will need to become familiar with correct grooming tools and the right way to groom your individual breed dog.

Do you have children? Are you planning to have children within the lifetime of your dog? I simply ask you to try to look into the future so that we can try to avoid possible heartbreak down the road. The more realistic you are in the beginning, the greater your chance of success.

Will your new dog have a "job"? Will he be playmate to the kids? Will he go hunting with the hubby? Perhaps you would like him to be protective. It is important to consider all that you need from your dog before you even bring him home.

I do not want to dissuade anyone who wants to give a good

home to a dog. Lord knows there are enough homeless dogs, so that even if everybody adopted two, we would still be in dire straits. It is imperative though that we understand the requirements of what makes a good home and realize that it is not just a place to eat and sleep. More than that, your home should symbolize family to your dog.

I feel compelled to tell you about the first incredible experience I had with dogs, which changed the entire direction of my life. I can remember the boxer that I had when I was only three years old. Perhaps it was my mom telling me when I was a bit older how this boxer, named Spice, found her in the local supermarket. I had fallen and cracked my head open on the sidewalk outside our summer rental. Since Mom hadn't left a very capable baby-sitter with me, the dog did what had to be done—found my mom and brought her home. Needless to say I survived the fall. This is just the first personal experience that I can recollect. There are many more, some of them truly amazing to me.

I remember hearing an old Native American folktale. When God created the earth, he placed all the animals on one side and all the people on the other, facing each other. As the earth started to part, the dog jumped over to the human side. The moral of the tale being that dogs are great friends to humans and humans can be great friends to dogs. I often wonder who benefits from this contract more, them or us? The tremendous benefit to you, as a dog owner, is almost incalculable. Studies suggest that heart rate and blood pressure are reduced as a result of contact with dogs. Dogs guide the visually impaired and are trained to help the hearing impaired. Police agencies use dogs for a variety of tasks including patrol work, narcotics searches, explosive detection, as well as search and rescue operations. Dogs are used for therapy involving children and senior citizens. Service dogs aid in the mobility of the wheelchair bound. I could go on to elaborate on the efforts of working dogs, sheepdogs, hunting dogs, guard dogs, sled dogs, and most commonly, companion dogs. Dogs have created quite an impact on civilization as we know it. It is easy to see the positive effects they have on us. I wish I could say that we had the same positive effect on them.

Ninety-one thousand dogs are euthanized every year. There is something ethically and morally wrong with this astonishing statistic.

These creatures, who are simply following their instincts, are being destroyed for being themselves. We helped through selective breeding to make them who and what they are. For example, if a breed is developed for pulling sleds, it is wise to assume that this breed will forge on a leash. Therefore, if you need a dog that walks quietly at your side, perhaps a sled dog is the wrong choice of dog. Many dogs find themselves in shelters because their owners did not understand them. These dogs may have been inappropriate for the living situation that ultimately housed them, which caused problems for their owners, therefore causing problems for themselves. It is sad that with all the information available about the propensity of the various breeds and sound training principles, that we continue to put to death so many of our canine friends.

When you finally ask if you should be a dog owner I hope you say yes because you relish the thought of sharing your life with a dog. The responsibilities will blend into what will eventually be one of your greatest rewards. For me, it has been one of the greatest pleasures in life. The experience can warm your heart and touch your soul forever.

Why Would I Get a Dog?

I have often wondered what causes people to cohabit with dogs. Why is it that some people are willing to share a small studio apartment with a dog that is not even splitting the rent? I have witnessed people obtain dogs to offset the loss of a loved one. I have seen dogs brought home for the enjoyment of children. I know dogs who have become surrogate spouses and surrogate children. There are dogs with daily jobs to perform as their life's work. Additionally, there are house dogs, yard dogs, guard dogs, competition dogs, and companion dogs to choose from. Why would you get a dog? Perhaps you are looking for a jogging companion. Maybe you want a friend to watch television with. It feels really good to have someone at home anxiously awaiting your arrival. You are "Superman" to your dog. Your dog thinks that you are the greatest thing ever created. You take care of him and love him. And he knows it. It's hard to turn your back on that feeling. But never forget your responsibility, it's part of the bargain.

What Responsibilities Are Associated with Dog Ownership?

Think of yourself as a "doggy" employer who happily pays their wages. You joyfully provide housing and medical benefits. As part of your benefits program, you will offer excellent nutrition, exercise regimens, and continuing education. If it is beginning to sound like they have a great boss, then you are getting the idea. We must also provide the necessary legal documents as required by local laws. Mandatory proof of vaccination and license are often required. In chapter 2 I will discuss the specific responsibilities and characters of individual breeds.

How Do I Know If I Really Like Dogs?

Maybe you never owned a dog but have had some exposure to them. I guess you like being around dogs or I suppose you wouldn't be reading this book. Now, let me offer a few suggestions on how you might be able to get a little dog savvy before you bring one home.

Find a shelter in your area and volunteer a few hours a week to assist them with the care of the homeless dogs. Volunteers are also often accepted in veterinary facilities, dog training classes, boarding kennels, and grooming shops. Another helpful test is to pet-sit for a friend—this is akin to living with someone prior to marriage. Spending a little time around dogs before you bring one home is a great way to begin, and it may make the difference between success and failure.

Does Everyone in Your House Like Dogs?

Be thoughtful in your decision. Does Grampa live with you? Will your elderly mom be okay with a dog in the house? Is she allergic? When you are not home, who is caring for your "baby"? Is the person who is home all day with Fido able to handle him and are they treating your dog as you would? Is the time reserved for training your pup being taken up by your five-year-old son? How do you convey the magnitude of the responsibility to others involved in this project? In the dog world, inconsistent treatment breeds bedlam. You must make sure that everyone in your home is prepared and anxious for the total package before the little darling arrives. If the family is ready and everyone in your house likes dogs, then congratulations are in order.

Will the Dog Like Everyone in Your House?

Although you have arrived at the decision to get a dog, you should now consider that dogs can be equal to humans in terms of the amount of affection and attention that fulfill them. Each dog has his own threshold though. I have seen dogs solicit attention and then after accepting several strokes, lunge to bite. I have experience with dogs that are great with kids, but the parents may encounter aggression when they try to discipline their dog. On the other hand, it is not uncommon for me to see dogs that are great with adults but have problems with kids. The relationship between kids and dogs fluctuates, as each matures at a different rate. Dogs generally have a difficult time with toddlers, yet some dogs love toddlers and distrust teenagers. Dogs are honest creatures. If you see a problem with an antisocial dog, then you may need to return or "re-home" him and find a less suspicious candidate for your home.

Once you get the right dog, one who is sound and friendly, then you can move along. Let the dog show you who he is, and you will teach him all he needs to know about who you are as a family.

What Are the Dog's Needs?

There is a fallacy that states that small dogs are better in apartments because they require less exercise. The truth is that small dogs tend to be more active than large dogs. They may be down close to the floor, but they are busy. Small dogs tend to bark more than many large ones, and this can often be linked to a lack of exercise. I had a client tell me that she did not exercise her small, young, very busy terrier because "the park was dirty." I told her, "Dogs like dirt." She replied, "Concrete is our cup of tea." "The park is dirty" is a bad excuse for not taking your dog out. Even if a dog is paper trained to eliminate in the house, that doesn't suggest the dog should not be exercised. Lack of outside activity can manifest in problem behaviors such as tail chasing or obsessive licking as well as antisocial personalities.

Many breeds are very easy to care for with minimal effort concerning grooming and training. Others are a bit more involved.

However, learning who needs what usually comes from living with your dog and understanding his individual character. Thus, nothing is more important than good research into breed histories and character. It is well known that beagles are relentless when they get on a scent of a rabbit. If you think that calling him off the trail without having him on a leash is easy, think again. If you are attracted to beagles and live in a city apartment, you will want to think about how you will be able to effectively exercise him without taking the leash off. I am not suggesting that he can't be trained. It's just that some training exercises are more difficult than others when we begin looking into the idiosyncratic breed dispositions.

Exercise, good food, a clean dry place to sleep, health care, plus grooming and training are going to be the overall considerations. However, one of the greatest needs your dog has is companionship. Your dog's emotional health is dependent upon the quality of the time you spend together.

What Tools Are Necessary to Raise My Dog Well?

If you are going to build the perfect dog, then you may need a few tools. A leash seems to be the one piece of equipment that accompanies dogs worldwide. I always advise my students to have leads of various lengths for training.

There are many varieties of collars and harnesses. Knowing which device belongs on the body of your dog may be confusing. But the proper use of this equipment is essential for correct training.

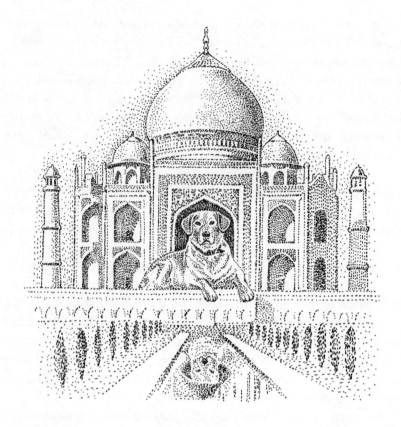

Treats are often used as tools in dog training. I have found human food to be extremely effective in gaining a dog's attention. Hot dogs, cheese, cereal, and carrots top the list of favorites.

These days, dog crates are very popular because they help facilitate early housebreaking. They are available in a wide variety of sizes and may be made of wood, hard plastic, or wire. The last type may come with an optional divider, which allows you to increase the space of the crate as your dog grows. When purchasing your crate you may want to buy the size crate that can accommodate your adult dog. The plastic crates are generally less expensive and are approved for airline travel. However, if your puppy is of a breed that will grow to be large, it may be necessary to purchase several of these plastic carriers while your puppy is growing. Therefore, it is imperative that you research the most cost effective choice that will fit your lifestyle. These plastic kennels are easy to clean and stack up when turned into themselves. I have seen these crates turned into doghouses by removing the door. The bottom half of this crate may be turned into a comfortable bed by placing a blanket or pillow in it.

Dog crates are designed to contain puppies and dogs while their owners are away from the house or unable to supervise their activities.

Crates also influence housebreaking by limiting the puppy's living space. Dogs naturally keep their living space clean. Over time, a puppy's crate time is decreased and his free time increased as maturity and training take hold.

If you choose to have a doghouse, then the climate that the dog will have to endure will help in making the best choice of building materials. Look for a well-insulated house that is easy to keep clean and keeps your dog free of wind and rain. The doghouse should be off the ground by a few inches and provide adequate ventilation.

Toys are important because dogs have a natural desire to play, and if you fail to provide the toys, they will discover that your personal items can be used as their playthings. Some dogs like to chase, some like to chew, and some like to jump. Finding the right toys for your dog can make the difference between appropriate chewing and massive destruction. I have seen dogs that jump seven feet into the air for a Frisbee and dogs that will swim to retrieve a ball or Kong toy in the water. I have also seen dogs leap in the most natural way over fences that come between them and a satisfying game of chase-the-squirrel. Toys will fulfill his drives and increase his desire to see you as his caregiver. You will no doubt be amazed at the numbers of items out there for dog owners to buy for their beloved pets. Buy wisely and have fun.

Can I Be Certain That This Will Be a Positive Experience?

No. You cannot be certain of anything other than what you see at the time you are seeing it. We humans have not mastered the science of looking into the future yet. Dogs do not come with guarantees. Marriage has the same uncertain future, yet every day countless couples embark on the voyage. But at the point when a marriage goes bad, although there is tremendous hurt, it was a decision made between two parties who have control over their own futures.

Remember that when a relationship between dog and owner goes bad, the dog has no control over his destiny. If you end up giving him to someone who you do not know, how can you be sure they will keep him safe and well for the rest of his life? You can't. And let's agree that moving a dog from home to home is not the best life for him.

Nobody can guarantee that this is going to work out, but the same can be said of most things. Therefore, give it your best shot and make sure you are serious about the commitment. Then you can honestly say that you gave your all to a worthwhile cause.

2.

The Selection Process

How to Choose the Right Dog

Remember all those reports you had to do in school? I did them on the American Kennel Club groups of dogs. I can remember my fifth-grade teacher asking me if I might be interested in another topic. I felt obligated to say yes, so my next report was on sports. I did a paper on racing greyhounds. All those years I've spent studying the breed standards since then combined with my exposure to the majority of dog breeds enables me to shed a little light on your possible selection.

The right dog can be found when you do your homework. People often come to me with the wrong dogs and ask "How come I ended up with the wrong dog, despite the fact that I did the research and talked to the breeder?" Unfortunately, for breeders love makes them blind when discussing their breed. This bias makes it difficult for potential new owners to obtain a reliable assessment from breeders. Usually, owners get the whole lecture on how the dogs they work with are perfect specimens and the characters of their dogs are beyond reproach. Books written on specific breeds rarely mention the shortcomings of the particular breed discussed. Thankfully, there are those who are more interested in the welfare of the breed rather than the economic advantages related to the release of their book and subsequent puppy sales.

It's difficult to know whom to ask for advice in these dog matters. Everybody who has ever had a dog feels like an expert, and these people love to talk about their dog experiences to anyone who will listen. I love dog stories too, but that's not the kind of help you need right now. The most unbiased advisers are veterinarians and dog trainers. Call a few of them and ask what they think about the breed that you are interested in. Also, call your local shelter and inquire about which purebreds they see brought in most often. This will let you know how difficult owning certain breeds can be. There are many factors to plug in here. My local shelter currently has approximately seventy-five pit bull terriers housed and awaiting adoption. This is a lovely breed of dog, but oftentimes misunderstood. Many local municipalities are passing breed-specific ordinances making ownership difficult. Special insurance policies, limited leash length, and mandatory muzzling when in public are making certain breeds less popular.

When a breed loses favor in the public eye, it's sure to become a regular at shelters. Ask yourself if you are prepared to make the commitment to an attempt to overturn public opinion.

Where Should I Look for a Dog?

Dogs may be found from one end of the earth to the other. Where do you find your canine soul mate? He may be found at a breeder, at a pet store, in a shelter, or chasing a bus down the street. Although it may seem as hard as finding your human counterpart, the following will hopefully provide a network of information resulting in your finding a right dog.

Breeders

When searching for a reputable breeder of purebred dogs, you should look for one who has a good track record. If they breed working dogs, then they should have produced many dogs that have earned working-dog titles in their specific area. If they breed for conformation (body structure), then they should be proud to tell you of the many champions in the pedigree of your potential dog.

Breeders of show dogs frequently predetermine the destiny of their puppies prior to sale by specifically placing their puppies in show-homes only. A show dog breeder may choose to deny sale of a quality puppy to a family that has no intentions of showing the pup. The same can hold true for a working-dog breeder. The number of titles a dog achieves measures the success of the breeder. Titles also help to legitimize their breeding program.

Pedigrees When you purchase a purebred dog from a breeder, papers from a registry are furnished. In the United States the American Kennel Club is the registry most often used. Breeders have two options available to them. They may either allow full registration or limited registration of each puppy in a litter. Full registration allows for future breedings with registration of the puppies. Limited registration prohibits the registration of future puppies. Full registration is permitted to those puppies that appear most correct. Puppies with serious faults should be given limited registration papers. In any case, a pup or dog with a pedigree is traceable in terms of lineage.

When a puppy is sold that clearly has faults in conformation and/or character, the new owner has to be responsible enough to understand that their beloved pet should be neutered or spayed. This in no way is a negative reflection on your family dog. Some of us know when our dogs have enough good traits to warrant passing them along. If you are not sure, a qualified breeder can help you by looking at your dog and its pedigree. A breeder can even make specific recommendations on which lines may complement your dog's bloodlines. In the case of a family that is not interested in showing and breeding, then it would be an economically sound choice to pick the less expensive pup in a litter.

I wish I could say that all breeders were honest, but I have seen mixed-breed puppies sold for what a purebred show quality puppy would sell for. When I see the numbers of poor quality puppies being produced and then hear the price tags on them, it infuriates me. When the general public comes to realize that just furnishing a pedigree does not make that pedigree worth having, then perhaps we will begin forcing dishonest breeders to stop breeding dogs altogether. I met an Australian terrier pup in one of my puppy kindergarten classes. This dog had been sold with registration papers as a Yorkshire terrier but was without a doubt an Australian terrier. His owners became skeptical of his heritage when every Yorkshire terrier they saw was smaller than their puppy. Their little guy had a different texture to his hair coat and an unusually shaped head, and his body was longer than that of any Yorkshire terrier they had ever seen. When I showed them a picture of an Australian terrier, they seemed relieved at knowing what they had. What about his papers? All I can say is that this situation is not as uncommon as it should be.

On the other hand, in terms of inherent characteristics, it is no surprise that progeny resulting from dogs with thunder phobic behavior will exhibit the exact same behavior. Of course not every puppy produced by a thunder phobic parent will be symptomatic, but some will. It is therefore my opinion that these dogs should not be bred. The behaviors of your puppy become more clear when you know the parents and grandparents of your pup.

A knowledgeable dog person reads a pedigree with the ease of an average person reading the morning paper. When requesting the assistance of a breeder in pursuit of a puppy, you should be prepared with a couple of questions:

- "What was your goal for this breeding?"
- "Have you ever bred these two dogs together before?"
- "If this is a repeat breeding, what positive traits were seen in the first breeding?"
- "What negative traits were seen?"
- "Would it be possible to talk to an owner of one or more of your dogs?"
- "How long have you been breeding dogs?"

- "How many different breeds are you currently breeding?"
- "Are you a member of your parent breed club? If yes, for how long?"
- "What information is available on the sire and dam?"
- "What information is available on the grandsire and grand-dam?"

Taking the initiative to present these questions creates an atmosphere of professionalism and hopefully puts you on a more equal footing with the breeder.

The help of an honest and knowledgeable breeder can be tremendous when choosing your puppy. They have been watching the development of the pups and are aware of their individual behavior patterns.

Pet Stores

Puppies are sold in stores and malls nationwide. Because it is not publicized well enough, I will say that puppies should not be bought from these places. The dogs are placed behind glass enclosures further contained in individual cages. Many of these puppies live through their entire critical socialization period in this environment, with very little opportunity for adequate interaction.

In all honesty, I have trained some very nice puppies purchased from pet stores, but I have also seen the worst-case scenarios from these pet shop puppies. All too often irresponsible breeders do not breed true to the standard of their breeds. These puppies are often mass-produced to be sold for profit only. Overbreeding can create puppies with physical faults and temperament problems. Odds are you can find a better candidate through a reputable breeder. All too often puppies are purchased from pet stores with the term "kennel club" in their titles. Do not confuse any pet store with the American Kennel Club, which is a registry in the United States. The AKC does not sell dogs.

Shelters

As a young child, my mother would take me to animal shelters all around New York City. We didn't have much money, and these visits were an interesting and inexpensive activity. The funny thing is that I was getting an education and didn't even know it. We often stayed at the shelter for hours at a time, and after a brown-bag lunch in the car, we would go back into the shelter to watch the dogs or visit the feline adoption area. We saw dogs found on the street, dogs dropped off by their owners, and dogs with litters of puppies. I saw just about every type of character imaginable and successfully owned quite a few of these dogs and cats along the way.

How Do I Find a Shelter? Shelters are everywhere. Almost every town in the United States has at least one. Shelters advertise in the local newspaper or in free weeklies. Supermarkets sometimes hang posters with a few pictures of homeless animals available for adoption at the local shelter. Police departments also can direct you to a local animal welfare agency.

Are All Shelters Alike? No. Some shelters provide temporary housing for the homeless animals in their city while others attempt to provide long-term solutions. Temporary housing forces euthanasia of unadoptable pets. However, when a shelter has a no-kill policy, the number of homeless dogs continues to rise daily, and with an ever escalating population how can shelters provide effective long-term care?

At a recent summit held in New York City, Sue Sternberg, a notable dog trainer, said that the maximum number of months acceptable to house dogs in a shelter setting was five to six months. She added that there were frequently irreversible behavioral changes after that period. Therefore dogs should not spend over five to six months in a shelter, and unadopted dogs must be reevaluated at that time.

Bitches versus Dogs

One primary question I am always asked is "Which is better, a bitch or a dog?" On one level, this is an easy question, but on another level, it is a very difficult one. I am the guy who always says find the right individual by its character—who cares what gender it is or even what it looks like? That was the easy answer. The difficult one is deciding on male versus female, with the understanding that dogs are generally larger than bitches and often more aggressive. There are pros and cons to both genders.

Bitches

I personally have always preferred bitches, but I have also experienced a few male dog relationships over the past fifteen years that were as warm as the ones I have ever had with the bitches. I still tend to recommend a bitch over a dog to homes with children. Perhaps there is some maternal quality in many bitches that keeps me feeling this way, or maybe it's just that we had so many great female dogs in our home over the years.

Do not become too concerned over the heat cycles and feminine problems because you will spay your girl, and that's that. It's a bad excuse for you to say that "she is going to bleed all over my house," because if she is spayed, she won't bleed a drop.

Bitches can be almost as behaviorally challenging as dogs. A tough girl is as least as tough as any dog—sometimes even tougher. The bottom line for me is still to support bitches as a choice when there is a question in your mind as to what to choose. I believe that getting a bitch stacks the odds in your favor that your dog will make a positive contribution to your entire family—*almost* like a second mom.

Dogs

Although I love male dogs, they can be a handful at times. Males are famous for doing a disappearing act when your neighbor's female dog is in season; this wanderlust can get owners into trouble. Males are also very willing to fight with other males in defense of their territory or a female "friend." Male dogs tend toward territorial urination, which shows itself through leg-lifting behavior. Leg lifting of itself is usually not a problem unless it is occurring in your home.

I love male dogs because they are a ton of fun. I have had a few rough-and-tumble types to play with over the years. I have found these males a bit more active with greater endurance than many of my females. Males are also considered by law enforcement to be the choice for service jobs.

The positive attributes of the male may actually be considered negative traits to inexperienced hands. Again, the bottom line here is to find the best dog based on its good behavior.

Mixed Breed versus Purebred

Mixed-Breed Dogs

Mixed-breed dogs can be equal or superior to purebreds. The significant issue to the average owner generally is whether or not the individual dog is a correct match. When there is no future in the show ring or when the dog is being obtained as a pet for the home and family, then the pedigree of the dog usually becomes less important.

Dogs of questionable heritage are often immunologically very strong. Charles Darwin felt that random selection created the strongest type. This does not make purebreds weak, but mixed breeding tends to reduce the problems associated with inbreeding.

I have successfully trained as many mixed-breed dogs as I have purebred dogs. There are fewer certainties associated with the characters of mixed-breed dogs, simply because of the lack of genetic histories, but some of my most successful training students were dogs of questionable heritage. Some of them were trained as service dogs or for family protection as well as pet-facilitated therapy. Mixes can have all the workhorse enthusiasm of the true working purebreds, but once again, the key is choosing the correct individual.

A mixed-breed puppy grows less predictably than a purebred in his size, weight, and coat type. His temperament will be the result of his environment as well as of his unknown heritage. He will be a clean slate for you to build the perfect dog.

Only when choosing a mixed breed as an adult can you clearly know what you are getting in terms of size, weight, and coat variety. This is a big help to those of us with restrictions. Although many dogs are not so quick to show you all of their temperament, a knowledgeable eye can also see the general character of an adult dog. Dogs will often change after a bonding period takes place. Fearful dogs sometimes become more confident, and confident dogs sometimes become even more confident.

Purebred Dogs

The advantage of a purebred dog is that you can pretty much predetermine its size, color, hair type, and general character.

Be aware that being purebred brings the positive heritable traits along with negative heritable traits. For example, a problem that is well known by the dog world is an orthopedic condition called hip dysplasia. Although it is found in a few medium-size breeds, hip dysplasia is most common among large-breed dogs. There are many idiosyncratic ailments associated with purebred dogs. Generally, in an attempt to decrease these organic heritable diseases, the specific breed clubs offer suggestions on specific tests to determine if a dog is breedable. Another

example of a negative heritable trait is Progressive Retinal Atrophy (PRA) in Labrador retrievers. Qualified dog breeders certify the eyes on their breeding stock in order to limit the occurrence of this disease. The breeders of breeds known to carry hip dysplasia certify their breeding stock with the Orthopedic Foundation for Animals (OFA) and/or with the Penn Hip procedure in order to minimize the incidence of hip dysplasia. Genetic testing for inherent diseases is on the brink of becoming available to breeders, which would make certain diseases be problems of the past.

Breeders of purebred dogs are responsible for attempting to breed their dogs to the standard dictated by their national breed club. When all goes well, lovely dogs of correct type are provided. It is imperative that breeders have a thorough grasp of genetics. While line breeding is used to create what is known as "type," it can occasionally result in problems. Fresh bloodlines should be introduced from time to time. This area is best left up to professionals, but form should always follow function in the purebred dog.

I have seen many beautiful purebred dogs with correct characters end up in shelters because their owners did not understand the breed's true nature. When form follows function, a border collie cannot be an apartment dweller. A purebred that had been bred for conformation (body structure) may be a different story. I can't remember seeing a rough collie that would have the propensity for sheep herding. The instinct for work has long been bred out of the vast majority of these dogs.

The lesson here is that if you are looking for a pet that will need to be calm indoors, don't get a sporting dog that comes from a working-dog line. In the sporting/hound and working/herding groups, breeding kennels can be located that would be specific for breeding either working-dog or conformation (show) lines. The intent of breeders in a perfect world would be to unify both elements and have working temperament in a show dog body. I wish I could say that I've seen this element, but I rarely do. Usually I see one or the other, and what is more interesting is that they are usually placed in the wrong home. It is like a bad dream when working pedigrees are placed in homes of families that have no idea what their busy dog is trying to do. Show lines typically have fewer working drives and therefore tend to make easier pets. A dog that has drive for his intended work should be worked, which allows the dog to fulfill his instinct. You should understand the instincts of the breed of your choice to insure his proper handling. If you have chosen the correct breed for you, then successful ownership is in the cards for both you and your dog.

Rather than naming every breed in each of the groups, I have chosen the more popular breeds and given a brief behavioral description based on my experiences with them. My findings with the various breeds are a result of training sessions, behavioral consultations, and of my work as a veterinary technician. My contact with dogs over the past many years has been constant and intense, and as I continue to learn and teach, my passion for dogs and their behavior remains strong. I hope you value my experience and that it helps you find and build the best dog you have ever had.

Sporting Dogs

Cocker Spaniel
This popular breed can be wonderful when well bred. On the other hand, the cocker spaniel can be a nightmare when it is not. While I have seen severe aggression in this breed, I have also had wonderful training experiences with cockers. They are bright and willing to comply to their owner's direction when trained.

English Cocker Spaniel
This is a lovely breed of dog, though much less popular than its American cousin. The biggest problem I have had with this breed is the housebreaking issue. I have also trained a few nervous dogs of this breed. For the most part they have shown themselves to make very nice pets. I recommend this breed to apartment dwellers with the energy to accomplish the housebreaking. Once the initial training is done, this is a really nice dog.

English Springer Spaniel
Slightly larger than the cocker, the springer is also a very nice breed for those who are considering a medium-size dog with moder-

ate exercise requirements. Unfortunately, the springer is also known for having serious aggression issues. Dominance aggression is not uncommon in this breed. It is believed that one or two show dogs in the past that were heavily bred passed this tendency along. If you choose the springer, get a guarantee on character as well as health, because when you get a good springer, you have a great dog.

Brittany Spaniel

I love the Brittany spaniel. I have trained many over the years, and they tend to exhibit excellent character. They are adorable as puppies and keep a young dog's attitude throughout their lives. They are easy to train except when the "come" command is used in the presence of distractions.

The biggest problem that I have encountered with these dogs is their tendency to run away. They are an excellent problem-solving breed, and this translates to "watch the latch on the gates." Your dog will figure out how to open them and you will be running to the pound to retrieve your dog so keep identification on your Brittany spaniel. Consider this breed for active households.

Welsh Springer Spaniel

Generally smaller than the springer, the Welsh tends toward having housebreaking difficulties but also tends to be low on the scale of aggression issues. It is important to exercise this active breed.

Field Spaniel

I have trained a few field spaniels and found them to be consistently active and bright dogs. They clearly need exuberant exercise, and if not sufficiently exercised, they are no fun to be around. Great breed for those who like hiking and are skilled enough to train this breed to come when called.

German Shorthaired Pointer

This is one of my favorite sporting dogs. Both sexes are generally terrific. I have trained a few females for clients and then wanted them for myself. I find them to have a lot of energy, yet be calm and quiet indoors. I have seen these dogs show protection of their families without being dangerous and continue to be wonderful around children. They need daily exercise. Frisbee works well for them, or just throwing the ball around suits them just fine. Although not a city-type breed, I've seen them do well when their exercise and play drives were fulfilled.

German Wirehaired Pointer

My experience has shown me that they are harder to train than the shorthair and tend to be a bit more nervous. In the right hands this breed can be a star. But these dogs can be stubborn and aggressive in the wrong hands. They need early training and socialization in order to increase the odds for a positive relationship.

Pointer

The pointer is a nice breed, though I have trained only a few that actually lived as pets in homes. The pointers that lived as kennel dogs for hunting were usually as lovely in their personalities as the house dogs. I had only one case of aggression with the breed and I'm certain it was the environment, not the dog. A very nice sporting dog.

Labrador Retriever

This breed is billed as a very popular dog for the kids. I find Labradors run the gamut from the very best to the absolute worst. So many energetic working dogs end up in homes with very young children, no yard, and no way to channel their drives. I have seen severe aggression in hyper field dogs and poorly bred show dogs alike. Puppy mill puppies are to be closely looked at for signs of early dominance before being brought home to the kids. Signs of early dominance include mounting, excessive biting, demanding barking, and guarding food or objects. Labradors are a nice choice when they are well bred, well raised, and well trained. They are the potential best of choices when these elements are secured. When considering a Labrador, keep in mind that the dog needs a lot of time, exercise, play, and training. My own caseload suggests that the black dogs train most readily, the yellows next, and the chocolates follow last. I can only speculate on this phenomenon in that when one breeds specifically for color, the character will eventually suffer. I am looking forward to the time when breed clubs begin cracking down on poor breeding practices and creating continuity in this majestic breed.

Golden Retriever

The golden retriever was once upon a time my standard recommendation to a family with young children. I am a little more careful these days. The average family can easily manage a golden when the dog is what a golden should be. A golden should be friendly under just about all circumstances. I have seen children tormenting goldens, yet the dogs almost enjoyed the rough handling the kids put on them. I have seen goldens bothered to the point where most dogs would have swallowed the kids, but the golden would tolerate it. In my mind this is what the golden is—a breed for the home, a breed for the kids, a dog with energy but not out-of-control excitement. A very trainable breed that tends toward compliance.

In the past six years or so, I have noticed a surge in the golden popularity. I have also noted that with the increase in numbers, there has been an increase in possessive aggression. Many dogs are now guarding objects from their owners. This is not appropriate golden behavior, and the quality breeders of golden retrievers will attest to that. Many possessive aggressive puppies seem to grow into dominant adults. This is not a surprise, but aggression within this breed is a surprise in itself.

I will pass along an observation that I noticed in my practice. The dogs with very red coats and those of questionable heritage appear to be more problematic than the golden- or the wheat-colored dogs.

Flat-Coated Retriever

Other than finding a couple of flat-coats a little soft in their characters, I really like this breed. I find them to be nice pets in suburban settings and are generally good with strangers and children.

As always, training and exercise help make this a somewhat easy breed to live with.

Chesapeake Bay Retriever

This is a large, hardy breed for the person who likes to pal around with a nice strong dog. I would be really hard-pressed to place this breed with an inexperienced handler or with very young kids. They are beautiful, full of life, intelligent, and active. This breed could easily be trained to protect the family. In the wrong hands this breed could develop an aggression problem within the family. All things considered, in the right hands, a nice breed.

Irish Setter

The Irish setter is a beautiful dog. I have had many opportunities to train this breed and have found that when they are fulfilled in terms of exercise, they are terrific pets. However, when they are neglected, they are a sad sight as well as destructively, almost compulsively, active, and nervous. I have had aggression issues with several members of this breed, and they will scare you, should you ever see an attack by an Irish setter.

It is imperative that they be heavily exercised. That means you will be heavily exercised because they will not do it themselves. They enjoy the company of their handlers.

English Setter

The English setter is also a very beautiful dog. My overall experience with these dogs tends toward working pedigrees. Generally, working dogs are a handful because they are athletic and energetic. The English setters I have trained were bright, easy to train, and extremely compliant. I had two or three females present with minor housebreaking difficulties.

I must say that I have dog trainer friends who have worked with dogs of show pedigree and claimed to have tremendous difficulties with getting the information into the heads of these conformation giants. I am just passing along what a few great trainers passed along to me. Clearly, each individual is to be carefully examined before being accepted as your new dog.

Gordon Setter

The Gordon setter is less commonly seen in my area. I have trained about four dogs in the past twenty years. Not much to base an opinion on, yet I recall all four were alike. They were whimsical. I know that is a bit of a cryptic description, but whimsical is the right word. "Out there," "in the wind," and "airy in the mind," are what my experience with these four Gordon setters was like. They slowly learned their basic manners and went on to enjoy family life.

Vizsla

The vizsla is a nice breed for those interested in keeping busy. I have seen this breed become relatively quiet as they mature, but when they are pups, they need substantial exercise in order to "keep the peace." I have found vizslas easy to train, basically requiring a consistent obedience foundation, coupled with a short play period after the training session. Many vizslas will be happy to perform simply for the play period that follows.

I have seen only one or two cases of aggression in this breed, and they appeared to be a result of too little exercise and inconsistent training.

The hair coat is easy to care for, and in general, it is a breed void of many inherent physical problems.

Weimaraner

The weimaraner is a large gray dog with an outstanding affinity for training. Exercise and grooming requirements are similar to those of the vizsla. I have trained many weimaraners with terrific success. They tend to be good family dogs, yet those individuals that are high-strung should be carefully monitored while in the presence of children. The weimaraner generally has a somewhat active defense response, therefore it is quick to respond to stimuli. A stable environment is essential for this breed.

Hounds

Sight Hounds

Afghan

The Afghan is a gracious-looking breed of dog that possesses the remarkable ability to ignore its handler when distracted by moving objects. I also have had noncompliant behavior with a few individual dogs that were presented to me for basic training. Food-motivated training generally went well, but there would always be a show of defensive aggression when a failed exercise resulted in even a mild leash correction. As beautiful and feminine as these dogs are in appearance, they can be aggressive. Exercise is imperative in the ownership of an Afghan hound. Bred to sight and chase game, they are serious when it comes to their jobs. Not a city dweller, unless you are training yourself constantly for the New York City marathon.

Borzoi

The borzoi is a large, graceful, and lean breed. My experience with them tends toward more problem behaviors rather than basic obedience. I have had to help owners try to teach their dogs not to run away or simply come when called. Also I have had several borzois with dominance aggression issues. Borzois can be gentle dogs, but they can also be nervous dogs. It is important to fully understand how much stimulation your individual dog can accept prior to teaching the basics. This is not a first dog for a family.

Scottish Deerhound

A large, very nice, gentle breed of dog. The Scottish deerhound is a lovely choice for the family that likes hiking and long walks.

I have found them to be a generally well-behaved breed. Occasionally they are a bit slow to housebreak and are not always super in obedience. They are very willing to comply when it comes to the important things. I have never had a case of aggression with the deerhound, and I wholeheartedly recommend the Scottish deerhound as a family dog.

Greyhound

The movement toward humane treatment of these fine yet often abused runners has helped us to see many more in the cities. I have trained many greyhounds and have found them to be very quiet in the home environment. They appear very stoic and gentle until you take them outside and watch them chase down a rabbit or squirrel.

I had a client in New York City with a rescued dog. Every morning she went out to Central Park for their morning walk. Just about every day this dog would in a flash poke his head into some bushes and come up with a rat. Needless to say, my client was a little taken aback by this daily event. We easily "fixed it" by teaching the dog to focus on the owner instead of the bushes. It took several weeks but the natural chase behavior lessened over time. This does not mean that the dog will never chase again. It simply means that we can control this instinct through conditioning.

The greyhound may run away if given the opportunity, so leash walks on long lines are the way to go. Fenced-in yards are nice too. Remember they will do well in an apartment situation if given regular exercise. I love the breed.

Irish Wolfhound

The Irish wolfhound is another wonderful dog. Everyone seems to know that this is usually considered the largest breed of dog. With this in mind, studio apartments are out. They do not seem to require much exercise but they can enjoy a good run.

I visited the home of a single woman who resided in a suburban neighborhood. She had nine Irish wolfhounds in her home. The house was clean and the dogs were all happy and friendly. The reason I was called out was to observe the dogs for possible aggression among themselves. There was none. They did play rough, and this concerned the owner enough to have me come out and look at it. I understood her fears while I enjoyed the sight of these huge dogs frolicking around her yard, jumping on one another and growling in play. My job in that case became not one of dog training but one of owner education.

I have trained quite a few Irish wolfhounds for the nuclear family with great success. I have on occasion seen nervous individuals, so be careful when picking your puppy. No one needs a nervous dog the size of a small car.

Saluki

I have been around very few salukis, but the dogs I've seen were nice, easygoing individuals that possessed nice character. They have a tendency toward active defense response, so it is nice for them to have a consistent environment to live in. The least amount of stress works for them.

Exercise helps to make this a very nice breed.

Whippet

I have found the whippet to be one of the most aesthetically stunning of breeds. They are simply gorgeous. They may be a bit difficult at first to housebreak, but with patience and consistency you will succeed. I have had a little difficulty in teaching basic obedience to whippets. They seem to dislike the "sit" command, which may be related to their high tail set. When the tail on a dog is set high, sitting may be a bit more difficult although very possible. Consider this as a possibility before you become angry at your dog for sitting slowly or not sitting at all on command.

Scent Hounds

Basenji

This African barkless dog is a very interesting breed. They are compact, very "neat looking," and are a very nice dog for apartment dwellers. I have seen some examples of aggression and housebreaking problems in the basenji.

This is a hunting breed, and this fact should not be ignored. Leash walks are sufficient for basenjis. They really like to play, so make the outings good. A very bright breed, they seem to excel at problem solving more than obedience.

Early training helps to center this breed, and consistent signals are imperative when attempting to get the basenji to work.

Basset

This low-to-the-ground hound dog is famous for his adorable looks. With his ears hanging down to the floor and tail always held way up in the air, there can be none cuter.

The basset is famous for being one of the most difficult breeds of dog to housebreak. I have encountered numerous cases of dominance and territorial aggression in this breed. I have also trained a few really sweet bassets, but even these angels were a wee bit loose in the housebreaking department.

Home owners with doggy doors are best suited to this breed. Bred to follow their nose to eternity, a fenced-in property is essential when housing a basset.

Beagle

Beagles are clearly one of the cutest breeds when they are puppies. They too are sized well for apartment dwellers.

I have seen many types of problems associated with beagles. I have seen separation anxiety problems, barking problems, and problems with housebreaking. Beagles will also usually eat anything not nailed down and will run away if the opportunity should present itself. I have even counseled beagle owners whose dogs displayed territorial aggression issues.

Beagles truly do not belong in a city atmosphere and should be in the field chasing rabbits, not in the living room getting fat on a couch.

Should you choose a beagle, select a breeder that breeds for your needs. Beagles with show bloodlines often have considerably less working drive and energy; they are therefore easier to manage in close quarters. Working-dog kennels should produce a loud and energetic dog. Working bloodlines will produce rabbit-chasing, trail-blazing puppies. It's not a good idea to blaze trails on your living room carpet, so select your puppy with care.

Bloodhound

The bloodhound has endless energy. I remember Duke, the *Beverly Hillbillies* bloodhound on TV, always just lying around the front door, looking very lifeless. What a well-trained dog he was.

These dogs will track until they drop. Many police departments are going with the bloodhound for tracking lost children as well as escaped criminals. I read an article once about the bloodhound and its amazing powers of tracking. One police officer was quoted as saying, "They have the IQ of dirt." But though there is Jell-O in the head there is genius in the nose.

One Manhattan bloodhound was nervous and seemed not to be fulfilled with respect to exercise, even though his owner did the best he could, given the constraints of city life.

The suburban dogs were a bit better, when a large yard to investigate was available for them.

This is a great and noble breed of dog but not suited for everyone.

Coonhounds

Coonhounds are a terrific hunting dog with nonstop drives. It is a beautiful breed that is absolutely not for the city. Even in the burbs, if you can't adequately exercise a coonhound, it's best to leave them in the hands of a qualified hunting dog trainer and seek out another breed choice.

Dachshund

The dachshund comes in two sizes and three coat types. They may also come in a few different colors. The two most popular are black/rust and red/rust.

When I was a young technician, a gifted, slightly older, and more experienced technician told me that I was not allowed to favor or discriminate one breed over another. She said it was unprofessional to victimize any breed and that the owners pick up on your prejudices rather quickly. There would be no faster way to lose a client than having them believe that you disliked their breed of choice. In the same breath, she also said, in her infinite wisdom, to watch out for little red dachshunds, they have a strong tendency to bite.

I have found the little red doxie thing to ring fairly true. I have trained a fair number of what turns out to be my wife's favorite breed, the dachshund. These adorable little guys can have a big-dog attitude. It takes that kind of temperament to ward off a badger, which is the job that dachshunds were bred to do. Dachshunds are often long on self-expression and short on compliance.

They can be a bit noisy and will alert you to most any sound produced by man or beast, making them very good watchdogs. Problems may occur when this overprotective behavior is allowed to manifest itself without owner influence. What I am saying here is, if you want a friendly dog, you must help to teach your dog what is okay with you. If barking is undesirable, then you must consistently teach your dog to remain quiet when he alerts to sounds outside your home. When guests come over to visit, your dachshund should be a social member of the group. Therefore you must insist on his good behavior in their presence. I have seen so many cases of territorial aggression in the dachshund resulting from lack of proper socialization or appropriate training.

The dachshund is a tough candidate for your average family but is also a clown of a breed with tremendous temperament and a loving disposition.

Norwegian Elkhound

I have trained many Norwegian elkhounds with great success. They can be lovely dogs. They do have a heavy coat, with a very thick undercoat, that requires regular brushing in order to keep well groomed.

I have seen two or three cases of dominance aggression in the Norwegian elkhound.

Overall, I have found this breed to be well focused but a bit stubborn. However with consistent training, this is a splendid breed not requiring an excess of exercise.

Rhodesian Ridgeback

The Rhodesian Ridgeback is interesting in that I have observed severe and dangerous aggression from a fair number of male dogs. I have also seen aggression in the female but with considerably less frequency.

I have a friend with a large male Ridgeback that is about four years old. Jesse is a very big baby with dogs, cats, and kids. If his female owner were being attacked, he would genuinely be concerned, but not enough to help her by showing aggression.

A large lion-hunting breed, you must be careful when selecting a Ridgeback. I have had owners that were "in the pet care business" and had irreconcilable aggression problems with their otherwise well-trained dogs.

Working Dogs

Akita

The Akita is a majestic dog bred by the Japanese to hunt bears and guard. They are large, substantial, quiet, and clean.

The problem with the Akita tends to be related to territorial aggression. I personally have experienced at least a dozen cases of ter-

ritorial aggression in this breed. I have testified in court numerous times in bite cases involving Akitas.

The Akita is definitely not a breed for the average family. I have seen severe aggression in both male and female Akitas. I watched a spayed female Akita in Manhattan go to urinate on a garbage bag and lift her leg as high as any male dog I have ever seen mark an object. I wanted to run home and get my video camera. She was an interesting "girl" to say the least.

I have seen an occasional Akita that was not just quiet but also had enough threshold to maintain a friendly disposition. Many of the Akitas I have trained with, including two Japanese imports, had very little tolerance for prolonged petting. They tended to prefer quiet verbal praise over being petted.

I want you to fully understand the nature of this big and beautiful breed. They can be friendly puppies and still grow to be difficult to manage as adults.

Alaskan Malamute

The Alaskan malamute was bred as a sled dog. I feel as though this should say it all, but many people without adequate housing still insist on keeping these dogs as pets. Some breeds are just not made to be housebound companions.

A special-needs dog is how I think of malamutes. They are very nice to have around when you have the room for them. A potential owner should be comfortable with the concept of living together with a mutual respect. Those into the dominance thing should be careful when attempting to dominate a malamute. They may not be very tolerant of being rolled or shaken.

Bernese Mountain Dog

The Bernese mountain dog is a large breed of dog whose character may resemble that of the golden retriever. I have trained a fair number of these dogs, and when they are outgoing and friendly, they are among the best of family choices. On the other hand, when they are nervous, they are nightmares and unfortunately, I have run across a few with extremely weak nerve thresholds. When any large breed of dog is chosen, it needs to be well behaved and well socialized. When you find a nice Bernese, you've got a great dog.

Boxer

A well-bred boxer is a wonderful family dog. They have a coat easy to care for, are not too large, and tend to be well behaved with children. The boxer is an easy breed to train. Although generally friendly, it commands respect because of its size and square face. This is a very jumpy breed of dog, so if you choose the boxer be prepared. The naturally active boxer needs quite a bit of exercise in order to maintain a relaxed demeanor.

Bullmastiff

The bullmastiff is one of my favorites. I have never trained one to unusual heights, but it can probably be done. Bullmastiffs are just plain nice, easily cared for, slow-going, beautiful dogs. Most examples are tight lipped, so the saliva is not all over the place, as is true with other mastiff dogs. I have never had reservations in recommending the bullmastiff to any family that had the space to house them properly.

Doberman Pinscher

The Doberman is a dog that has suffered from an unearned reputation of aggression. The fact is that they are almost everything but. I have observed a couple of cases of aggression in male Dobermans but have certainly seen more examples of this behavior in Labradors.

Dobermans train as if there were some genetic predisposition toward the training itself. They are extremely sensitive and at the same time more defensive than the German shepherd dog. They have a very warm and responsive character. They always seem to have their heads somewhere on your body, or at least one part of their anatomy is touching you.

I have personally owned this breed a couple of times and trained many more. I respect and admire the Doberman.

Giant Schnauzer

The giant schnauzer is a large, very classy, and elegant breed of dog that carries itself proudly in conformation and character.

The giant schnauzer needs grooming to maintain the coat type. They are a bit stubborn yet are very bright and train well with consistent handling. The male can appear a little sharp at times, showing his readiness to react to any adverse situation. I have trained this breed in obedience and found them to be quite responsive to consistent training. This breed may possess enough initiative to run a household. Although they are nice, they are best housed by experienced enthusiasts of giant schnauzers.

Great Dane

I have seen all the problems that life has to offer the Great Dane, both physical and behavioral. The sheer size of this breed brings with it orthopedic and systemic medical trouble. When there is an aggression problem in the Great Dane it is further complicated by the dog's size. Obviously, if you are bitten by a dog of this size you are likely to have severe injuries.

I have very successfully trained many Great Danes and they were a pleasure to work with. I have counseled many Great Dane owners whose dogs presented aggression and phobic difficulties, and enjoyed good success. Not a breed for the first-time owner; this is a prince of breeds when the genetics are correct and the dog is in the hands of a capable owner.

Great Pyrenees

The Great Pyrenees is a very large white dog bred to ward off wolves and guard sheep in the mountains. If you do not have mountains in your backyard or wolves to scare off of your property, carefully consider the job that your dog may take in its place. Clearly, a seasoned handler is necessary here. I have had numerous dominance cases with this breed because the handlers were not strong enough.

Kuvasz

I have had two occasions to train this breed. The two were alike, except the female was sharper and more aggressive than the male. (The male was no joke either.) He was tolerant of my presence but could have lived without knowing me. They appeared loyal to the owner but were not very social, thus making my job a bit difficult. I was able to positively influence both dogs to some degree. Not a breed for just anybody, the Kuvasz needs a committed owner, particularly when not in working situations.

Mastiff

I once met a 260-pound male English mastiff that didn't like kids. When the woman opened the front door with the dog at her side, I was stunned at how large he was. When I realized there was no leash on this guy I became a bit nervous, knowing there was an aggression problem. I lived. He didn't like neighborhood kids, although he was fine with the three children in the family. I plotted a course of controlled social visits to the local playground. Using positive reinforcement the conditioning worked well. He soon became more than tolerant of the children—he actually would seek them out for a treat and in return behaved appropriately.

I also volunteered, wearing a body bite suit, to take a couple of chomps from an English mastiff. They can run fast and bite hard. I got knocked down to the ground, and it hurt. They possess the ability to make ominous protection, but when this breed is of sound mind they are really quite nice.

I trained a few nervous males and females, so be careful in your selection of an individual puppy and socialize this breed early.

Newfoundland

The Newfoundland is a super nice breed when you have the space for a dog of this size. I have found them to be relatively easy to train and pleasant to be around. The attention-needing Newfoundland enjoys contact with their owners and are not kennel-type dogs. They like long walks and swims in the ocean, lake, pond, pool, or puddle.

My preference tends toward the black dogs over the Landseer, among whom I have had a couple with questionable characters. They were nervous, defensive types that couldn't be trusted around children.

Portuguese Water Dogs

This breed is one of my favorites. The Portuguese water dog is so easy to train that they have caused me to laugh out loud on more than one occasion. I have shown some of these guys an exercise just once and they come right back with it. They are simply unbelievable.

They can be very mouthy puppies and consequently difficult for a while with small children, but if you manage them well as puppies, then it should work out fine. I find this breed active and extremely playful, which are two positive characteristics when considering training.

Some Portuguese water dogs have shown me independent behavior, while a small number of males have been seen for aggression.

I highly recommend this breed as a family dog, considering their need for exercise. The coat requires care, but the upside is they tend to be hypoallergenic for those seeking out low-dander pets.

Rottweiler

The rottweiler is the epitome of the high-defense breeds. These dogs were produced by the Romans to pull carts, herd sheep, and guard. They are terrific at these jobs. They are not, however, the best pets in the world unless you are prepared to train and maintain them.

Interestingly, on the whole I have found the female rottweiler to be just wonderful. The females are family oriented and generally sound with children. On the other hand, males are usually the opposite. Males are generally quiet and clean about themselves and their environment but the problems I've seen with them are always aggression related. Dominance and territorial aggression run rampant in the male rottweiler. I have trained a few German imports and have actually found these males to be not only more physically athletic but also more behaviorally sound. I have had only two or three cases of aggression in the female rottweiler, and I attributed all these cases to inconsistent handling.

I am okay with aggression in this breed because they should be aggressive. It is what they were bred for. I have seen male rotties vie for physical attention by nudging a visitor's hand, but when the visitor complies and is about to pet the dog, it attacks the visitor.

Please consider your own skills as a dog trainer, as well as your housing responsibilities, before you go out and buy this truly wonderful yet very serious breed of dog.

Saint Bernard

The Saint Bernard is a very large, wonderful breed of dog that requires work. One must adequately socialize a Saint Bernard puppy in order to help it achieve a friendly and outgoing disposition. I have counseled Saint Bernard owners with terrible aggression problems in both the male and female.

I can't recommend this breed for a first-time or even second-time owner. This breed is best suited for an experienced handler with a large yard.

Samoyed

The Samoyed is a beautiful dog. They are very bright and energetic when they are not allowed to become overweight. I have had so many positive training experiences with them when the owners were able to be clear and consistent.

If not fulfilled in terms of quality time and exercise, the Samoyed can bark a bit and run away if given the opportunity, become aggressive, show destructive behavior tendencies, and dig up the yard. A beautiful and sensitive breed, they are terrific at problem solving. A Samoyed will get your attention when it wants something. An owner of a Sam will tell you they are work, but they are worth every minute of it.

Siberian Husky

The Siberian husky is incredibly smart, quick to train in obedience, and absolutely gorgeous. This breed is compelled to run. If the opportunity presents itself, they will jump over or dig under your fence in an effort to escape. Even in the suburbs, this breed is a tough candidate. The Siberian husky was bred to be a pack animal, so imagine the level of energy it takes to pull a sled across the tundra. Consider the drive and determination that these dogs demonstrate in their propensity to work and know that this breed will require a large well-enclosed yard. These dogs thrive on contact with their owners, and because they are accustomed to working in packs, they tend to be very social.

My advice to those considering a husky is to be prepared to spend a great deal of your time exercising your dog. It is painful for me to see Siberian husky puppies cooped up in cages at the mall. These dogs are unlikely to find suitable homes because they are difficult to appropriately place. Problems with Siberian huskies include barking and howling, digging, dominance and territorial aggression, food guarding, and predatory behavior. Unless you live in Alaska, think three times before you bring home this blue-eyed beauty.

Standard Schnauzer

The standard schnauzer is a nice breed of dog that is very trainable and void of many congenital problems. They are strong, active dogs that tend to be great pets and offer a bit of protection for their family. Early training is recommended in order to establish a proper relationship with them. If all the elements are present, this breed makes a nice picture.

Terriers

Airedale Terrier

The Airedale terrier is a large dog with tremendous play drive. Exercise is imperative for this breed. Should you attempt to cheat your dog out of running, he will climb the walls. I have enjoyed working with Airedale terriers and have found them to be comical, energetic, and easy to train. This breed is also very capable of protection or police work. Airedales require regular professional grooming, and many are actually plucked instead of cut. A well-groomed Airedale is a happy Airedale.

American Staffordshire Terrier

The American Staffordshire terrier is a close relative to the English Staffordshire bull terrier. Similar to the American pit bull terrier in appearance, this breed is AKC registered. The American pit bull terrier is still often bred for its fighting drive. The American Staffordshire terrier is more commonly bred for the show ring. As with all dogs, there are exceptions. I do not mean to imply that every American Staffordshire terrier will be gentle and that all pit bull terriers will be aggressive. Everything considered, I recommend this breed for its loyalty toward family and its desire to comply.

Australian Terrier

The Australian terrier is a spunky little guy that is lively, stubborn, smart, adorable, and often slow to housebreak. It takes an assertive owner to command the respect of an Australian terrier. I have marveled at the fine performances offered by this breed at obedience matches. Once you have earned his respect, you have gained a great little dog.

Bedlington Terrier

The Bedlington terrier resembles a lamb, is as stubborn as a mule, and is as cute as a bunny. I recently worked with a lovely young female Bedlington that trained like a dream and captured my heart. She was great with the family and possessed the uncanny ability to read their minds. Some have a genetic predisposition to liver disease, but it is important to know that diagnostic tests are available in order to rule out this problem in your potential puppy.

Border Terrier

The border terrier is a wonderful, playful, very bright little dog that, despite its need for exercise, makes a great apartment dog. They tend to be tolerant of children and have a seemingly endless propensity for all types of training. I highly recommend the border terrier as a family dog. The border is energetic, so daily exercise is essential to produce a well-mannered pet.

Bull Terrier

The bull terrier is generally recognized as the dog of General George Patton or as Spuds McKenzie. This breed is known for its aggression toward other dogs and small animals. They do however tend to have good relationships with children because they perceive the youngsters' vulnerability. I have trained many bull terriers in obedience with good success. Unfortunately, obsessive-compulsive behaviors have been noted in this breed, which can be exhibited as tail chasing, obsessive licking, and self-mutilation.

Cairn Terrier

The cairn terrier is a popular and favorite choice of breed, if not because of Toto in the *Wizard of Oz* then because of its compact size. I have had difficulties with aggression and housebreaking in this terrier.

When the cairn is well trained, it is a true pleasure to live with. A warm and personable breed, it can make a great dog for kids.

Dandie Dinmont Terrier

I have trained three Dandie Dinmont terriers. Two were easy. One was a pet store puppy that was presented with elimination problems. All were very cute and capable of good obedience. They were all stubborn but eventually trained well despite this streak.

Fox Terrier (Smooth)

The smooth fox terrier is a smart, quick little dog with tremendous energy and play drive. Basic training generally goes very well.

Problems usually stem from aggression to other dogs and cats, which is a result of their innate drive to hunt and kill rats.

Fox Terrier (Wire)

The wirehaired fox terrier is a great little breed that is similar to the smooth fox terrier in character. I have experienced very enjoyable training sessions with wirehaired terriers and found them quite easy to train. When we have a consistent owner, we usually have a well-behaved dog.

Problem behaviors may include digging, excessive barking, house soiling, and aggression. They also will run away if given the opportunity.

Irish Terrier

The Irish terrier is fairly well known for their persistent dog aggression. I have successfully trained this breed in obedience, and many of these dogs were very easygoing individuals. I have also had several cases of aggression in the Irish terrier. Their personalities are somewhat childlike.

Kerry Blue Terrier

The Kerry blue terrier is a beautiful, stately type of breed that is very energetic and generally full of piss and vinegar. Once the primary relationship issues are resolved, this breed may excel in basic obedience. To achieve compliance, it is important to teach the dog the structural hierarchy in order to gain his respect.

Known for their tendency toward dog aggression, Kerries can live in harmony with others.

Lakeland Terrier

I have a great admiration for the Lakeland terrier. They hardly touch the ground while running full gait, but given appropriate exercise, they may be housed in apartments.

The Lakeland may bark excessively, be a bit troublesome to housebreak, and show territorial aggression while simultaneously achieving the status of the most delicious of breeds.

Potential owners of Lakelands must have energy and patience so that they can successfully train their puppy.

Miniature Schnauzer

The miniature schnauzer is a wonderful breed for adult families. The schnauzer makes a good watchdog by virtue of its sharpness and tendency to bark. The miniature schnauzer may also be good with children when exposed to them as a young dog, but this breed tends to be too brisk and a bit lively for children.

Norfolk Terrier/ Norwich Terrier

The Norfolk and Norwich terriers are great little house dogs. My biggest problem with these super guys was correcting car-chasing behavior. They are so highly prey driven that they will run after just about anything. The funny thing is I have seen them placidly coexist with cats. As with just about all terriers, they can dig forever and seem to enjoy the sound of their own bark. Also, housebreaking may take a little patience on the part of the owner.

Scottish Terrier

The Scottish terrier is a feisty little guy with very large teeth. I have found the females to be less aggressive than the males. Although I have seen territorial aggression in this breed, the type of aggression I have most commonly observed is dominance aggression.

I had a Scotty years ago named Shamus who was totally friendly and totally wired. Living with him was a blast.

I have not encountered house-soiling problems in the Scotty.

Skye Terrier

I have had limited experience with the Skye terrier. The few I have worked with seemed a bit intense and had very active defense responses. I wouldn't recommend this breed for kids.

Soft-coated Wheaten Terrier

The soft-coated wheaten terrier is a very popular breed of dog. I have trained these dogs with ease in obedience and find that they enjoy the work. Wheatens require exuberant exercise and are less active in the home when that regular exercise is provided. The wheaten is considered a hypoallergenic breed that requires regular grooming.

The problems associated with the wheaten are many. I have had cases of aggression, house soiling, hyperactivity, excessive barking, submissive urination, and digging.

Staffordshire Bull Terrier

The apartment-size British variety of the American Staffordshire terrier is adorable as well as a great dog for the family. However, they may become animal aggressive as they grow into maturity.

Welsh Terrier

The Welsh terrier is a medium-size spunky Lakeland/Airedale look-alike. I have enjoyed all three breeds in training and found their characters to be similar in type.

Barking and digging may be behavioral issues associated with this breed.

West Highland White Terrier

The Westie is a very cute little dog often mistaken for a white Scotty. The Westie is a nice dog for older dog owners because it is small enough to easily handle. It has the spunk and personality indicative of a terrier. Also, this is a nice breed for a moderately active child because when called upon, they have great energy and love to play.

Toys

Brussels Griffon

The Brussels griffon is a delightful little dog. My experience has been great in terms of obedience, but the housebreaking has been difficult. Though they are small enough to be comfortable living in an apartment, they can go anywhere.

Chihuahua

I have always loved the Chihuahua. The training is always up to the owner, but I rarely find an owner willing to train a Chihuahua for obedience. This is a result of the incorrect assumption that a tiny dog is easy to handle. I saw a longhaired example floor the crowd when he performed in advanced obedience with an excellent routine.

Unfortunately, watching a Chihuahua in an obedience trial is a rare event. The majority of the Chihuahuas presented to me had aggression or elimination problems, and often at the same time.

The Chihuahua can be quite the barker as well, which makes this breed a really good watchdog. Although very small they are generally full of chutzpah. Good training prevents problems with this breed and should be started early.

Many Chihuahua owners keep these dogs in multiples. I have seen as many as ten in one home—a cute picture but very noisy.

Cavalier King Charles

The cavalier is a charming breed of dog. I often recommend them to families with children. I keep thinking about getting a cavalier for myself one day.

I have seen problems with shyness in too many individuals, so be careful when getting a pup. When they are well bred and have sound nerves, they are super little guys.

The cavalier may be a bit slow to housebreak, but be patient—you will eventually succeed. Medically, there is a tendency toward cardiac disease, so have your pup checked by your veterinarian immediately after he arrives at his new home.

Italian Greyhound

I have had many Italian greyhounds in my caseload. Most were seen for basic training, but some presented housebreaking and barking problems. In general, this is a very nice little dog.

Fragile in their bone structure, I would be concerned for an Italian greyhound in a home with young active kids. Clearly these dogs have energy and drive to play but can get worked up into breaking an extremity.

Maltese

Maltese are gorgeous little white longhaired dogs that require daily grooming. Early training should be sought in order to control their barking and overprotective tendencies against strangers.

I have found the Maltese to be very easy to train for general obedience and have trained many to use a litter box for elimination.

Miniature Pinscher

The miniature pinscher is an adorable little replica of the Doberman. Although they are not related, the miniature pinscher is the breed whose character is generally and improperly associated with the Doberman. The miniature pinscher is a sharp and tough breed of dog. Personally, I really like the breed.

This dog is not for just anyone. This highly spirited breed needs exercise and socialization during its initial critical socialization period (age seven to sixteen weeks). Early training helps to direct much of the pup's energy toward positive goals.

Papillon

In terms of its general character, the papillon is a very well-adjusted breed of dog. They are great at obedience training, tracking, and agility. They make excellent house dogs.

Pekingese

Occasionally a Pekingese comes through a training program with no problems, just routine obedience. I have always thought of the Pekingese as a nice dog. Sometimes, the explanation for a trainer not seeing a breed often is that the dogs are generally well behaved from the beginning.

Pomeranian

The Pomeranian is adorable and usually brilliant. I find this breed highly trainable.

If you are going to have a problem with a Pomeranian, it's likely to be barking or house soiling.

Poodle (Toy)

As with standard and miniature-size poodles, the toy is sharp-minded, quick to learn, and devoted to his owner.

I have always enjoyed the poodles in my class because they make the work look so easy. They would drive everyone else crazy. Owners of other breeds would ask me why the poodle can do it while their dogs couldn't. I would shrug my shoulders and say, "It's a poodle."

Pug

What a face! Nice lips! Seriously, I do love pugs. I have found the pug to be less vocal than many of the other toys, yet still energetic and fun.

The pug is a bit stubborn in obedience and a little slow in the house-training area, but with time and persistence you will prevail and become the owner of quite a cute and well-mannered pooch.

Shih Tzu

Although the Shih Tzu resembles the Lhasa Apso, I have found the Shih Tzu to be far less aggressive than the Lhasa Apso. I find them to be very willing to give focus and are, in general, a compliant breed. I have been successful in paper-training a moderate number of these dogs for city dwellers. This breed is sized well for apartment life. They are social, not terribly active, and warm companions.

This breed has been presented to me for house-soiling and aggression problems.

Yorkshire Terrier

I think of the Yorkshire terrier as a housebreaking nightmare. I have had too many cases to be kind on the matter. I think they have some sort of genetic predisposition. I have also treated many dominance aggression cases in the breed.

If you have a temperamentally sound Yorkshire terrier, you are surely blessed with the kind of relationship that will remain in your heart for a lifetime. They can be fabulous.

Nonsporting Dogs

American Eskimo Dog

The American Eskimo dog is a very bright and energetic breed. I have found them to be very easy to train in terms of basic obedience and trick work. Problems with the American Eskimo dog are generally centered around excessive barking and occasional dominance and/or territorial aggression.

Early training helps to ward off many of the impending problems associated with this breed.

Bichon Frise

These dogs are very popular because they are highly recognized as one of the hypoallergenic breeds. Many city dwellers prefer the small, clean, low-shedding breeds, such as poodles, wirehaired fox terriers, and Shih Tzus. The bichon frise fits this bill in a large way.

The bichon is relatively easy to train, except for house soiling, and can be a houebreaking disaster. I have noted that bichons that were house trained early later exhibited dominance behaviors.

Dominant puppies are often fastidious about their living space, which results in early housebreaking.

Boston Terrier

I love the Boston terrier and I have had many fun times training with them. True clowns, these guys are terrific, very quick to learn, and generally willing to comply. Problems are few with the Boston, but once again, I have found housebreaking to lead the list of possible troubles.

English Bulldog

The English bulldog is a medical nightmare. They tend to have bad skin, chronic bladder problems, mucous membrane irritations, and problems with their eyes. They have difficulty whelping puppies and generally end up being delivered by cesarean section. I have had several cases with dominance aggression problems. My experience has been that consistent training meets with positive results.

Chinese Shar-Pei

This Chinese fighting breed is famous for its wrinkles. Although they can be adorable, I have seen several dogs for aggression. For the most part, they are okay with family but distrust strangers and tend toward dog fighting and predatory aggression.

Shar-peis are not that difficult to train, but they can be stubborn. A balanced program of reinforcement is essential for the owner to achieve a social and well-behaved individual.

Chow Chow

The chow is quite a dog with its lionlike appearance and solemn attitude. It is one of the simplest breeds to housebreak. They are also usually quiet and not mouthy as puppies.

Chows possess incredible loyalty toward family members and oftentimes are dangerous to have around strangers. I have had a few cases of territorial aggression in the chow breed as a consequence of this loyalty to home and family, but granted, this is the focus of the breed. Should you choose the chow chow, early puppy socialization is the only way you can have a social dog. Should you fail to do this, your dog will love you but may eat one of your friends. Remember when you own a chow, it is normal for him not to tolerate strangers.

I have successfully trained this breed to do quite well in functional obedience.

Dalmatian

Firemen, popular movies, and their spots make Dalmatians a favorite of children.

The Dalmatian is an alert, strong, medium-size dog with great potential for just about any type of work. You should choose a job for your Dalmatian as it will be important in controlling your dog's energy and drive.

This breed is intensely eager to learn. While training with Dalmatians, I have personally learned a lot from them about reinforcement. This can be a stubborn breed of dog to work with, which is a very good thing for someone like myself who enjoys working out the kinks.

I have had many disastrous cases of territorial and dominance aggression in the Dalmatian. All too often this breed is selected for its spots—and there is more to the Dalmatian than just spots.

French Bulldog

An adorable, bright, feisty little guy, the Frenchie is cute. Be prepared to manage his possible dog aggression, but they are really nice animals.

I have trained with this breed many times and found them willing enough to learn the work. Sometimes they get a little spaced out, but usually their focus is great.

Keeshond

This dog from Holland is a cousin to the Pomeranian and other spitz breeds such as the Samoyed and Norwegian elkhound.

Nice family dogs, they can be a bit barky when not exercised enough. They are super house dogs that generally enjoy being brushed and pampered.

I have found the keeshond easy to train, and in general, a delightful breed.

Lhasa Apso

The Lhasa Apso is a shrimp in size and a giant in attitude. This Tibetan lion dog was developed as a guard dog, and its work ethic is holding strong. A furry adorable puppy shortly turns into something like RoboCop, leaving you wondering where that sweet puppy went.

Simple to housebreak, they are very clean dogs. Ninety-six percent of the Lhasas I've seen tend to bite. When considering this breed, be aware of these tendencies. Training as well as socialization should be started early. With the Lhasa your dominant status must be consistently maintained.

Poodles (Miniature and Standard)

Poodles are popular for the following good reasons:

1. Are very easy to train

2. Come in a size for everyone

3. Are basically hypoallergenic

4. Sport very fancy "hairdos" (haircuts and clothes)

The possible problems include aggression, house soiling, and excessive barking, although the majority of poodles are easily conditioned into correct behavior.

I have trained and counseled many poodle owners with the best of success and recommend the poodle for most situations. Buying a well-bred individual is the most important issue in poodle selection.

Schipperke

Schipperkes are interesting dogs. I personally like the look of this small, shiny, black breed. I also tend to enjoy a dog like this with spunk and spirit.

I have counseled owners on excessive barking, dominance and territorial aggression. This is not surprising, since they were bred to guard docks and barges. I have also enjoyed training the Schippy for basic obedience with great success. They are easily motivated with toys and treats and can train all day if they are having fun with the lessons.

Shiba Inu

Understanding this catlike breed of dog is the key to successful ownership. The shiba is a quiet and clean Akita miniature.

I have trained approximately ten shibas. All were aggressive. They all accepted petting for only a short time before they chose to walk away.

I have seen many shibas with low nerve thresholds and shibas with dominant characters.

A good shiba owner knows when and how to administer training and praise. The shiba is usually well behaved if not stimulated by an overzealous environment.

Tibetan Terrier

I have recommended the Tibetan terrier so many times for a variety of living situations. They are small, smart, a bit stubborn, and very cute.

Be sure to go to a reputable breeder when considering this breed. Although inbreeding is considered an acceptable practice, be careful to watch how genetically close the breedings are. Generally common relatives are four and five generations apart. Close inbreeding may produce serious faults in temperament, therefore it is always a good idea to look at pedigrees.

I have seen aggressive and phobic behavior displayed in the Tibetan terrier.

All in all, I find this a very nice breed. For the most part, breeders of Tibetans stay on top of their breed, keeping them physically and emotionally healthy.

Herding Dogs

Australian Cattle Dog

An active breed, the Australian cattle dog is intelligent and well focused. This would be consistent of herding-breed behavior across the board. A good choice for those with property and a propensity to exercise, I find this breed to be fine in suburban environments.

Australian Shepherd

Becoming somewhat popular these days, the Australian shepherd is a good-looking breed with boundless energy. The Aussie is also popular in the obedience ring, excels in agility, and makes a fairly good pet. I say "fairly" because they need a job. This is not the dog for the lazy man.

When not properly exercised, I have seen this lack of fulfillment result in increased aggressive behaviors. Lots of play is one way to keep his energy appropriately channeled.

Bearded Collie

I can hardly say enough good things about the beardie. When they are well put together in the head, they are amazing dogs. The beardie is a lively and well-spirited dog, with enthusiasm to learn and work. As with many of the herding breeds, they can be independent thinkers. This is not always good for the owner because the dog may elect to blow off a command and follow the beat of his own drummer.

It takes a little work to fully enjoy this type of "thinking" dog.

Belgian Malinois; Belgian Sheepdog; Belgian Tervuren

These three breeds are alike in terms of conformation, yet they have different characters. The Malinois's trainability and endless energy make it an unbelievable police dog. The sheepdog makes a beautiful show dog, carrying a long beautiful black coat. The Tervuren combines the two, with its long coat and some working ability in police-style work. All of them may excel in herding.

These dogs tend toward being on the sharp side, so it is imperative that no matter which of the three you choose, the individual is clear in its mind and has sound nerve threshold. This is necessary because if a dog is quick to make a reaction, we hope that its nerves prevent it from showing a highly defensive reaction to the initial stimulus. Balance of sharpness, hardness, and handler sensitivity are quality traits of the well-bred sheepdog.

I am friendly with several police canine trainers who work with Malinois and find them outstanding.

Border Collie

If you have the time, space, and energy to devote to a border collie, then this is a truly engaging dog. It is rare to find a breed that

possesses the continuity of the border collie. I have never seen a border collie that was difficult to train—maybe a few high-strung and
stubborn individuals, but never a slow learner.

Not a city dog, exercise is a necessity for this breed and ownership requires this commitment. New border owners are well advised
to "keep them busy, keep them entertained, or else they will destroy
your house." I personally have never found this to be the case,
although I can fully understand why these warnings are frequently
uttered.

Bouvier des Flandres

The Bouvier is a large dog originally bred for carting. I have
trained many Bouviers and have consistently found them to be easily
trained. The inclination toward protection training is evident from the
working bloodlines. The overall behavior from show bloodlines is generally soft and wonderful, and obedience tends to be easily learned.

This is not a breed for the first-time owner because they are large
and strong willed. A skillful handler though will enjoy the Bouvier.

Briard

I find the briard aesthetically pleasing. I like the beautiful long
straight coat. However, the upkeep is clearly a chore. Large and very
strong, this breed is not for the feeble and can take control of your life
using his intelligence and dominant tendencies. Become an accomplished dog trainer and you can enjoy one.

I trained with a seven-month-old French import. The bitch was a
nervous little thing and very sharp. At that time I was running a group
basic obedience class. When I began to place her into a "sit" position,
she bit me and held on to my hand. At this point, bleeding from one
hand and still holding the leash with the other hand, I pulled her off
and corrected her for biting and placed her into the sit. Today she is
one compliant pooch. The owner watched this event in amazement,
afraid that I was going to hurt his dog with a strong leash correction.
The dog was fine. In fact, the next week, the dog came running into
the training field so she could show me her excellent "sit."

I have had numerous cases of briards with defensive aggression
and been presented with several cases of shyness as well.

Collie (Rough)

The collie is a nice-looking breed made famous by Lassie films. Their hair is long and needs daily brushing in order to maintain healthy skin and a beautiful coat.

Although this breed was developed to herd sheep, it is my opinion that the working character has been bred out over many years. As a result we get a nice dog that is best kept as a house pet. The collie is a reasonable choice for those with children, a yard, time to keep up the grooming, and the energy to keep this breed occupied. I do not find the collie hyperactive, but if allowed to become bored, they may bark and whine in excess.

I heard a veterinarian once say half in jest that if a collie gets a bit of fecal matter stuck to his hair under the tail, he will die. The collie is a sensitive breed that benefits from close owner contact. They enjoy social activities with their families, including long walks, a game of fetch, or a nice long brushing.

I have trained many collies in basic obedience very well. Occasionally, I meet a collie that has a lot of energy for working, and in these cases, it really does not matter what style of work we choose, the dog performs well.

German Shepherd Dog

The German shepherd dog is my own personal favorite. I have owned and trained European imports and domestically bred German shepherds with great success.

The medical problems associated with this breed, though, are many. The standards for correctness are based on whether the dog is of working or show bloodlines. The breeders of working dogs prefer a straighter back, less croup. They feel that this creates a stronger rear and fewer problems with anal fistulas. Hip dysplasia runs rampant in this breed, and even the most well-bred dogs can be afflicted. The German shepherd may also have inherent health problems such as chronic colitis, epilepsy, and skin disease.

The character of a well-balanced, well-bred German shepherd dog is one of nobility and strength. When a German shepherd dog enters a room, he should create a noticeable presence. The breed should not be overly friendly or suspicious. They possess great ability in terms of training. This breed has a lot of initiative but is generally very handler compliant.

If the dog is a strict indoor house pet the double coat is a nightmare with its prodigous shedding and bountiful tufts of hair everywhere. You eat them, breathe them, wear them, and sleep in them. When the dog spends more time outdoors the shedding is less noticeable.

I feel that although this breed is generally easy to train, an experienced handler is recommended for the German shepherd dog because they are strong and can be menacing if not handled appropriately.

Puli

I have trained several puli over the years, and if nothing else, the experiences were comparable, males and females alike.

As puppies they are strong and bright. They are usually very clear in the mind, super in obedience, and often great in agility. If you like dog sports, you have a great partner here. Bred to herd sheep by jumping on their backs, they are bold little guys.

The problems I've seen all seemed to revolve around possessive aggression, but I have seen dominance aggression in the puli, as well. Training appeared to help across the board.

Shetland Sheepdog

Shelties are super nice little dogs. The well-bred Sheltie can excel in most canine sports. This is a wonderful breed in terms of a "good family dog."

The possible problems are excessive barking, house soiling, and aggression. The Shelties that have been presented to me for aggression generally showed territorial, not dominance-related, aggression.

Be sure to go to a reputable Sheltand sheepdog breeder because soundness is the whole shebang in a Sheltie.

Welsh Corgi (Pembroke)

Always nipping at you, corgi puppies are cute as can be until they start connecting with your skin a few times.

The corgi is bright enough to learn obedience exercises quickly. The key is getting this dog to be consistent, and I have had a little trouble with this part. The dogs seem to think they already know the job and go off to do it.

A breed with a lot of initiative, the corgi can be a bit willful and sometimes difficult to housebreak.

I have counseled owners in dominance aggression cases and I have seen interdog aggression, where they had to be separated from other family dogs in the household.

When they are good, they're great. When they are bad, they're very bad.

Miscellaneous Breeds

(I have trained various breeds not recognized by the American Kennel Club and thought I might throw in a few words on a few of these rarer breeds.)

Neapolitan Mastiff

The Neapolitan mastiff is not for just anybody. This giant breed is generally quiet but aggressive. If you own an aggressive dog and he vocalizes his intentions, that may not be an easy dog to own. Still this is much easier than the quiet dog who bites without warning.

I have seen a few Neapolitan mastiffs that were social, but the majority were good with the family and then very aggressive to visitors. When investigating an estate guard breed, look at the Neopolitan mastiff.

I have trained them for basic obedience with little or no problems but this is an immense breed with colossal strength and temperament, so be prepared.

Jack Russell Terrier

Bred as ratters, the feisty Jack Russell terrier is a huge dog in a small body. Potential owners should be clear on the activity level of the breed before embarking on what appears to be an excellent candidate for those living in an apartment.

The Jack Russell can be a problem around cats when not socialized early. I have had a few house-soiling problems with Jacks and have seen a few different types of aggression in this breed as well.

A skilled handler is best for this tough and extremely smart little dog.

Fila Brasiliero

I have only limited experience with the Fila. My experience dictates that only a skilled handler will be successful with a dog of this type. Certainly when a dog is appropriately placed, this will have an enormous effect on the overall behavior of the individual dog. When properly housed I can imagine that the Fila can be a loving family member, but the inexperienced should stay away.

American Bulldog

I have had more exposure to American bulldogs than many other rare breed varieties. I really enjoy this breed. The dogs I have trained were well balanced. Of course they are big dogs and require large or talented handlers, so consider the size and high activity level of these dogs. If you have a good training background and want a really nice breed, try the American bulldog.

Summary

The information in this chapter was written to help you choose the right breed of dog for your situation. I want to stress again that the success of your ownership relies on this choice. Beginning with the correct breed is crucial, but so is understanding how to assess the character of dogs in general. These are the keys to a lasting relationship.

3.

The Character of Dogs

Some authorities define *character* as attributes learned primarily in early life experience and *personality* as the combination of temperament and character. In general, temperament is thought of as whether or not a dog is well tempered or ill tempered. It is assumed that if a dog has good temperament, then the dog is nonaggressive. This is simply not true. In some situations, aggression can be considered a positive characteristic. Those "in the know" think of dog behavior in a much different way. We divide the character of dogs into two main categories, drives and traits. I was first introduced to this concept when I set out to select an adult German shepherd from Germany. I spent an enormous amount of time on the phone with a wise agent of German shepherds who taught me how all the drives and traits of dogs were ultimately used for training. The agent sent me a dog that she claimed had good character. So now that I had "talked the talk" it was time to learn how to "walk the walk."

After living with my new imported German shepherd for several months, I finally understood the importance of good character. The stable nature of this dog's personality was far more important than his formal training. This is what good character is. Some dogs have it. Some don't. However, most dogs have enough positive traits to build good character upon. When a dog has great character, he is respected by all that know him for his well-mannered behavior and seeming intelligence.

It is easiest to discuss the character of dogs while examining working-type dogs because they show their natural tendencies while doing their intended work. In most of Europe, working dogs are challenged to character tests, which are scored. If a dog cannot pass these tests, he cannot be used for breeding. His body may be perfect but still the dog will not be bred. I strongly support this philosophy.

Canine Character

The following chart provides as well as describes an array of canine characteristics. It will help you to understand how these instincts and traits are of value not only to your dog but also to your overall understanding of your dog's behavior.

Canine Character

TYPE OF DRIVE	TRAITS
Inherited motivation toward a biologic goal	Characteristics that modify drive-motivated behavior
Hunting	**Constitution**
Olfactory	**Courage**
Prey	**Hardness**
Retrieving	**Sharpness**
Play	**Temperament**
Social	**Endurance**
Dominance	**Intelligence**

Fighting

Territorial

Protection

Defensive

Avoidance

Sex

Nurturing

Drives

TYPE OF DRIVE	DEFINITION
Hunting	founded on the urge to satisfy hunger
Olfactory	the ability/desire to air and/or ground scent
Prey	the urge to chase, catch, kill, carry, and guard prey
Retrieving	expression of prey drive
Play	related to retrieving and social drives
Social	the urge to interact socially. Handler compliance, mimicking, etc.
Dominance	the drive for upward status
Fighting	eagerness to measure physical strength; pugnaciousness
Territorial	tendency to become attached to and defend a locality
Protection	the urge to defend pack members (family)
Defensive	the drive to avert harm through aggressive action
Avoidance	the drive to avert harm through avoidance behavior
Sex	the urge to engage in sexual activity
Nurturing	epimeletic (caregiving) and et-epimeletic (care-soliciting) behavior; also, nursing drive

Traits

TYPE OF TRAIT	DEFINITION
Constitution	physical attributes, condition
Courage	the fortitude arising only from constitutional and genetic factors; inversely, confidence is the fortitude arising from positive experience
Hardness	the ability to accept negative physical or emotional sensations without being momentarily or permanently influenced adversely by them
Sharpness	implies a low threshold for defensive and/or fighting drives, and also low thresholds in general (readiness to react)
Temperament	liveliness or alertness, and it is spoken of in terms of quantity
Endurance	based both on the dog's constitution and also in the general strength of his drives, desires, and urges
Intelligence	describes the dog's higher psychological and cognitive capabilities; ease of trainability

Drives and Traits

All dogs have drives and traits, although some drives are very strong in one dog and almost nonexistent in another. The behavioral character of your dog is based on these parameters.

Why do some puppies retrieve while others do not? Why, despite all the training to prevent aggression, is aggression still prevalent in dogs? Behaviors are the end result of the biological system. Basically, we can only behave in the manner that our bodies allow us to. In other words, we cannot flutter our arms and expect to fly. We like to think we have control of our dogs but our dogs, like ourselves, move through life doing actions based on biology and instinct and survival. When things are not going as intended, we are commonly led to believe that we have not sufficiently trained our dogs. It is not always about a lack of training, and it may be your dog's behavior that is creating the dilemma. Certain issues such as aggression, fears, and destructive behaviors are examples of problems often not resolved through obedience training alone. These situations affect the owners of all dogs, purebred or mixed breed, working dogs as well as pet dogs, males and females alike.

I hope that this information opens up a new world to you—a world that allows dogs to be who they are and teaches you to accept them and recognize the normal behaviors within them. This is a forgiving world for the dogs and their people who are desperately struggling to "get it right."

What Is Good Character?

Let's look at my idea of good character in a German shepherd dog. This dog will have strong retrieve drive, strong play drive, and strong hunting drive. A dog with low avoidance drive, low dominance drive, and medium defense drive is desired. Personally, I like strong prey drive, medium protection drive, strong fighting instinct, and strong nerves. I think dogs who exhibit handler compliance have high social drives, which generally creates a nice dog. This dog will have the hardness to deal with the kids running around the house with swords and will be almost amused at the prospect of a good fight and go for it with gusto when provoked. He will eagerly play tracking games, using his nose to recover hidden articles. A playful, outgoing dog who displays his ability to be friendly without being hectic and unruly around strangers is my kind of animal. My dog will clearly prefer his owner or family above any stranger. I like a dog that can recover quickly from a negative stimulus. For me, this is a good dog. However, it may not be a suitable dog for you, even if you are interested in German shepherd dogs.

Your main concern may be about your dog's conformation (body type). Or maybe you are very concerned about a correct croup (an area of the dog's back near his tail), while I don't give a hoot about his croup. If my dog has good character and a nice croup, super, but if his body is strong and the dog has no croup, then so be it. I'll still take him. Countless people appear to judge a dog's quality by the size of its paws. Examining the paws of a puppy in some attempt to clairvoyantly assess his eventual size and believing that he will be terrific simply because he might grow into a large adult is ridiculous.

The first quality you should look for while searching for your potential dog is *character*. This is not a book on genetics, but I think that Charles Darwin was correct when he said that natural random selection produced the strongest individuals. Although we can selectively breed dogs to show us physical and behavioral characteristics, every single puppy will have an individual character of his own.

When a new dog that is not a puppy comes into your life, your first impression may be that he is quiet and depressed. As a potential dog owner, you should be aware that it is possible that the dog will remain this way throughout his life. On the other hand, after a short "getting to know you" period, it is equally possible for this dog to become a lunatic. Frequently, dogs seem extremely placid after being boarded away from home for an extended time (three weeks or more). Some dogs are genuinely sensitive yet strong, while others are soft and emotionally weak.

Many dogs are just not confident enough at first to show their temperament. Nervous dogs are nervous dogs. I have seen numerous dogs with low nerve thresholds, and many tended to be sharp as well. This behavior was very much inherent in the individuals. Commonly, new owners of adult dogs believe that their dog's apparent apprehension is a result of previous abuse. This is rarely the case. The real deal is that these dogs have always acted in this manner. One of my criteria for a dog destined to live around children is that the dog must be able to readily recover from adverse stimuli. At some point, your children will surely be testing the nerve quality of your dog. Sharpness is the time it takes for your dog to react to a stimulus. On the contrary, hardness relates to the ease or difficulty in provoking a response. Sharpness may be considered a positive attribute in dogs bred to hunt small animals. The necessity for a fast reaction is "built" into these dogs.

If a seven- or eight-week-old puppy is active, outgoing, and friendly, it is unlikely that he will become fearful and nervous unless he becomes environmentally traumatized. If a puppy of the same age is already nervous, there is no real reason to assume that his nerves are going to strengthen over time. Training a dog with unsound nerves will not net you a super well-trained dog. If you need a retriever for some type of work, then be sure you pick a puppy with strong retrieve drives, or you may be struggling to teach your retriever to retrieve.

When you are evaluating a puppy, he is what he appears to be. There are no secrets. If it's a hyper little bitch yapping a million miles an hour, she ought to settle herself down by the time she is a senior citizen. If a puppy appears independent when you are around him for the first time, leave him behind and look for a puppy who shows interest in you. Don't choose the big active male in the litter unless you are prepared for the potential dominance and for all the time and training it could take to make him a great boy.

There are puppy temperament tests available to help define each character in a litter. I respect this urge but think that if we are attempting to gauge temperament in a scientific way, several tests would need to be performed to have sufficient data to prove consistent behavior patterns. The test itself may even cause unnatural results. You should just learn how to read dogs. Simply stand by and let them show you who they are. Believe me, they honestly will.

How to Recognize Drive— Reading Your Dog

Learning to read these drives requires you to begin making a conscious effort to take notice of the smallest of behaviors. Dogs' facial expressions change, as do their ear set. Although many assume that a wagging tail equates to a happy dog, this is not necessarily so. Dogs wag their tails when they are anxious or aggressive too. I'd like you to notice when your dog feels soft to the touch versus when he feels hard and perhaps tense. Watch the position of his head and how high or low it is held to know how secure he feels at any given time. I find it intresting to watch where a dog likes to position itself around his owner. This positioning shows me a bit about the relationship the dog and his owner have, as well as tells me a little about the independence and courage of the dog.

While running puppy kindergarten classes, I see puppies' personalities unfold before my eyes. In almost every class situation, at least one puppy will arise with his tail held high over his back as if it were the flag of his very own country. Sometimes these puppies will show aggression to other puppies when challenged to give up a toy or a good spot at the water bowl, while other puppies gladly give up their toys. Puppies will show shy, introverted behaviors as well. The trick to the apparent shy puppy is to discern whether or not this pup confidently chooses to back away from other pups or strangers or if the pup is genuinely insecure. To know which is which, watch the pup to see if it will go to others when treats are offered or if he runs up to other puppies when they are busy with still another kindergarten pup. Shy pups tend to be withdrawn regardless of treats and quiet class-mates. Watching and understanding these behaviors shows how choosing a puppy is a complex process. These natural behaviors are related to your dog's instincts and traits and will show themselves to you throughout the life of the dog.

Body Posture

It will be the posture of your dog that will show you what drive your dog may be exhibiting. As your dog chases a squirrel or a rabbit, his ears will be held forward until he gets near to it and then his ears will change to being held back away from the front of his head. These are natural changes that occur as his drive changes from prey drive to defense drive. Dogs will lower their front legs to the ground in a bow position to elicit play from others. Dogs retract their lips when they are about to bite or when they are stressed. Lip retraction is to prevent self-injury when biting, so it is a behavior to be aware of.

There is a posture called the submissive grin. My opinion of this grin is: if a dog is insecure, I would prefer not to positively reinforce the grin by laughing about it as if the dog were confident and happy. This behavior is best ignored. Dogs that are submissive will also roll over belly-up. This position, along with submissive urinating, is the ultimate surrender. These two behaviors are also best ignored when witnessed.

When confronted with a new friend, dogs will stiffen up, hold their tails high, and walk high up on their toes in an attempt to appear large until the structure of their relationship is worked out. It is also common for a dominant dog to place his head over the top of a subordinate dog's head or back. Posture is the key to reading dogs so keep an eye on the dog's body.

I used to belong to a dog training club. The dog sport being trained there was called Schutzhund. Schutzhund is a dog sport developed in Germany in the early 1900s originally designed as a temperament test. Schutzhund is a three-phase sport consisting of tracking, obedience, and protection. While in this club, we had a weekend seminar with a wonderful German dog trainer named Benno Golonska. Benno taught us how to use our own body language to more easily communicate with our dogs. He had the guys remove their baseball caps when they trained because the cap brim made it hard for the dog to see the eyes of his handler. Dogs read our eyes very well so it is crazy for us to make it difficult for our dogs to understand us, right? Right. When we stand up very tall or raise our arms above our heads and get "bigger," our dogs tend to stay a healthy distance from us. If we want them close, we must get small or low to urge them toward us and over time, with training and confidence, the dog will come close to us regardless of how "big" we are. Benno showed us how the slightest move backward made the dog move forward toward us. Benno gave us the idea of considering "who is the hunter?" and "who is the hunted?" This is a good question to ask yourself when being mouthed by your puppy. The fast withdrawal of your hands from the face of a puppy or dog is likely to bring their mouth right toward you. The opposite is also true; some dogs appear to be hand shy when a hand is quickly presented toward them. Body language is an interesting feature to study when you have a dog. The more you can see and understand about this paralanguage the better.

Vocalization

Dogs utter many sounds, so learning the qualitative differences among them is essential. Dogs bark and whine, yodel and growl. It is interesting to listen to one sound transform into another.

Canines are extremely vocal creatures. Howling and barking help each dog locate his pack members as well as identify the presence of nonpack members. Different tones emitted allowed clear identification of the intentions of each member.

There are several sounds emitted by coonhounds while they are hunting. Bawling is the sound vocalized when running, while a chopping noise is heard when a coonhound has treed a raccoon. I talked to a trainer of this breed and he told me of a transitional sound that these dogs make when they find a tree tagged (scented) by a raccoon and only chop when they actually tree the raccoon. During episodes of aggression, the sounds change as the dog's drives change from prey drive to defense drive. Dogs with serious civil (social) aggression will utter deep guttural sounds incorporated into the bark. The more you listen, the more you will learn.

Thresholds

One very important trait to note in dogs is their nerve thresholds. Threshold refers to the breaking point that produces measurable responses. Nerve quality is addressed in terms of thresholds. The ability to accept discomfort would be considered a high pain threshold. Psychologist Konrad Lorenz stated, "No behavior with a constant threshold has ever been observed in animals."

Perception of Vulnerability This is a trait that I think of as positive. This allows a dog to be able to discern children as nonhostile and small helpless animals as nonthreatening. A dogs that possesses perception of vulnerability is a dog that is destined to live successfully in a family with children.

Sound Sensitivity This is an important inherent characteristic. Sound sensitivity addresses the dog's ability to cope with loud souds. The problem is that many dogs do not manifest this behavior until they are middle-aged. Therefore it is welcome information when you can learn of this trait from the bloodlines. Obviously, when obtaining a grown dog of uncertain heritage this will be impossible, so it will be necessary to assess the dog's overall nerve quality. Dogs with very strong nerves are generally less apt to show sound sensitivity at any age.

Touch Sensitivity This trait is directly related to a dog's pain threshold. Touch-sensitive dogs are best trained either by luring and rewarding or by remote collar corrections. However, dogs with strong nerves are generally touch insensitive.

Courage This is a trait that arises from a dog's inherent ability to overcome strong opposition. Confidence, on the other hand, is a result of experience and positive reinforcement.

Fighting Instinct This shows a dog's tenacity and willingness to fight. This by no means suggests that strong fighting drive will produce a dog that would forge an unprovoked attack, but when provoked such a dog appears to be pleased with the challenge and is unafraid.

Sharpness This is spoken of in terms of readiness to react, or in having an active defense response. This trait is seen as a positive trait in dogs expected to do protection work. However, you can imagine where there might be a problem if a fairly sharp dog has weak nerves and great fighting drive. A dog that is quick to react and willing to fight but generally reacting out of fear is a big problem for the average dog owner. Unfortunately I've seen a lot of rottweilers that matched this description.

This chapter on character was a great challenge to write for me because learning and training with these principles forced me to look at dogs in a slightly different way. I was taught to believe I could train away any and all problems. This is not so. I have come to believe that what makes a dog good is good character, and many problems associated with dog ownership often reflect the poor characters of certain dogs.

Reading character is a science as well as an art. Practice by watching dogs work and play, and expose yourself to as many different breeds as you possibly can. Understand the nature of the breed you are interested in. Memorize their consistent behavior patterns, and be able to recognize their inconsistencies, in order to understand what's going on in their hearts, as well as their heads.

4.

....

How Dogs Learn

Learning will take place whether or not you train your dog. I recommend that since your dog is going to learn anyway, you might as well maximize on his desire and teach him appropriate behaviors.

From the start, it is of the utmost importance that he realizes you are first and foremost his friend. Next, you must understand that until you teach him any language, he does not understand your words. Oftentimes we seem to believe that dogs know what we want and are just being noncompliant. I personally would much rather assume that he either does not remember the command or he never really understood it in the first place. Noncompliance is not uncommon among dogs, yet it is always best to be forgiving whenever possible. It never does any good to assume your dog has a bad attitude or to assume one yourself.

Overall, canines do not care about words. Therefore it is important for your dog to be able to identify your attitude when you are soliciting him to provide a particular behavior. Initially, a dog attempts to assess his situation by what he senses. When you call him to come to you, is your voice encouraging or angry? Dogs prefer to interact with their owners when there is fulfillment for themselves. They are similar to children in that learning is best accomplished in a positive environment. This environment needs to be reinforced through sound teaching principles and procedures.

Principles of Learning

Classical Conditioning

Pavlov introduced classical conditioning to the world by pairing an unconditioned stimulus to a conditioned stimulus. The sight of meat was used as an unconditioned stimulus (ucs) for it produced salivation, while the sound of a bell was the conditioned stimulus (cs). After pairing the ucs with the cs, the sound of the bell elicited salivation.

Operant Conditioning

Operant conditioning is often called "trial and error" or instrumental learning. The behavior is the instrument that creates the reinforcement. Psychologist B. F. Skinner popularized a technique whereby when an animal presses a bar, it receives a reward of food or water. The initial pressing onto the bar was accidental but resulted in a reward. Thereafter each time the animal was placed in the box (Skinner box), the time spent getting to the reward lessened.

Counterconditioning

The goal of counterconditioning is eliciting a different response to a current undesirable behavior. If a dog who is shy around children is fed immediately upon seeing children, it will soon look forward to the sight of children, anticipating food at their very sight.

Desensitization

This process is utilized to reduce or eliminate reactive and/or phobic behaviors. Dogs that are frightened of going in a car first need frequent exposure to cars from a great distance. This distance is gradually decreased as the dog appears less stimulated by the sight of the car. In time, this dog will graduate to sitting in a motionless car and eating meals there. Eventually, your dog will be delighted to go for rides in the once feared car. This is a time-consuming but very effective process.

Extinction

Removing all reinforcement is the theory behind extinction. Excessive barking may be curtailed this way. If you do not react to or even acknowledge your dog when it barks, then the dog will eventually extinguish the barking. Prepare yourself for more, rather than less barking (extinction burst) because the dog will probably bark longer in an attempt to elicit a response from you. This is a principle that I have not had much success with.

Flooding

A horse was brought in by a neighbor who owns a wallboard firm. My training center is in an industrial part of town, and every day many eighteen-wheel trucks drive through. Initially this horse tried to run off from the sound of the trucks, but due to the sheer number of trucks coming through daily, the horse became comfortable within a matter of days. This horse was behaviorally flooded into habituation.

Frequently, dogs that are shy of other dogs become more social while being boarded at kennels while their owners are on vacation. The dog is desensitized by flooding due to the large number of dogs at the kennel in neighboring pens.

Punishment

Punishment is the use of an adverse stimulus in order to reduce the probability of a problematic behavior in the future.

Punishment is generally considered to be only marginally effective in dog training due to the time gap between behavior and reinforcement. An example of punishment might be: An owner comes home to find some shredded paper on the floor. He angrily proceeds to drag the dog to the mess and both verbally and physically reprimand the dog for the mess.

This dog will almost certainly be afraid of his owner's actions. This dog may show subordinate behavior or even aggression as a result of the forceful nature of the punishment. The dog may not make the association between the act and the punishment. The timing between events makes it extremely difficult for the dog to make a connection. In my opinion, punishment should be avoided whenever possible. Those who have used punishment as a training tool often say it rarely works out, admitting that the technique may not teach the dog anything and may very well cause conflict in the relationship between the dog and its owner.

Negative Reinforcement

Negative reinforcement increases a behavior while punishment decreases a behavior. Negative reinforcement has been a powerful and positive tool in the development of animal training over decades. The classic use of a training collar is a perfect example of negative reinforcement. When the dog pulls, there is discomfort, increasing the dog's desire to avoid the collar correction by walking near the handler on a soft nontaut leash.

Where We Begin

Focus

Before you can proceed to any basic training of your dog, you must teach him to focus. It is a good idea to begin your initial training by taking your dog into a quiet and familiar environment where he will be least distracted, thereby obtaining the greatest level of focus. Focus is the single most important command to teach your dog. Without focus from your dog, we cannot be certain we will elicit any additional behaviors. If your dog is looking away from you, he is listening to what he is looking at. Distractions are a large part of life, and you need to teach your dog to ignore them and pay attention to you.

More often than not, a new dog owner will ask me why they cannot simply use their dog's name in order to achieve focus. The answer is that on a daily basis, you will use your dog's name for many different purposes. Worse yet, you will probably yell his name at him when he is doing something wrong—much the same way your parents yelled your name at you when you were a misbehaving kid. Your dog is not a child, and if you scream his name at him in a harsh manner, he is sure to stop responding positively to his name.

The term you will use to teach your dog focus will be a consistently positively reinforced term. He will first learn to look at you on command no matter what is going on around him. Next, he will come to you when you call instead of running away off to who knows where. I know what you're thinking now. You think I'm crazy, that I don't know your dog, and there is no way that this is going to happen. So what do you have to lose in trying this procedure out? Every dog is different and I can't tell you how long it will take, but what else can you do with your dog that is low energy *and* educational? Here are the beginning steps necessary to teach attention.

Teaching Your Dog How to Focus

1. Begin training your dog when he has not had any personal contact with you for several hours. Mornings are great because you generally have had no contact with him overnight. A dog who has had minimal contact is more likely to want to give you his attention when the opportunity presents itself. Walk your dog before starting the session. Do not play with him or talk too much, just put him on a lead and walk him for elimination purposes. Afterward, take your dog back into the house so you may begin his training. Keep a leash on him so that you can retain an element of control.

2. We will be using food as a reward for this exercise. It is very important that you know what types of edible reinforcers will work on your dog. A hungry dog will be motivated by food, whereas a well-fed dog may show disinterest. Do not feed your dog his meal *before* training.

3. You will be teaching the dog to look at your face on command and a good reason for him to look at your face could be that there is great food falling out of your mouth. You could spit out little bits of cheese or hot dogs or cereal at your dog—whatever food works for him. Should this spitting trick cause unruly behavior or if your dog just can't seem to put the food together with your face, we can change the technique. If you have a small-breed dog or young puppy, you may get on your knees and show your dog a cracker hanging out of your mouth. When he notices the food, you can let him take a little bit from your mouth. The dog must be able to take this small amount of food gently, to prevent any accidental bites. If your dog is too rough in taking this treat, you may hold the treat in your hand, near your mouth, and give him small amounts as he looks at your face while giving the command. You must eventually be standing erect with your dog looking attentively at your face.

4. Typically commands such as "ready," "look," or "focus" are used. Any command you wish to use is fine, just be sure to be consistent with your terms. Your dog's name should be used prior to giving the focus command. Making a little clicking sound from your mouth after your command will help to teach your dog to look at you.

So, the order of the procedure is:

a. dog's name

b. command ("ready")

c. clicking sound from mouth

d. reward as your dog gives you attention

e. release from ready command ("okay" or "free")

Practice this constantly and reward your dog for it. Demand longer periods of focus, as well as focus with distractions. Increase the distraction level while demanding short focus duration. After you have achieved focus at high levels of distraction, such as someone calling your dog by name, or even someone touching him, you can move along increasing focus time. When commanded to look at your face, your dog must offer continued focus to you until released or commanded to the next task. Once you have established focus, the rest of your training becomes much easier because your dog is looking at you for direction. Since you have initiated your training with positive reinforcement, I must mention that although consistent reinforcement has been our order thus far, intermittent reinforcement is a far more powerful tool.

Reinforcement

Why is reinforcement so important? How will you know when to reinforce a behavior? Which type of reinforcement should you use and why? These are questions generally left unanswered, despite the fact that they are the most important questions people ask relating to good dog obedience.

Every day, owners ask their dogs to commit to a simple obedience exercise and get no response. The reason for the lack of response is lack of reinforcement.

Consistent Reinforcement This will teach your dog that when he shows you a correct behavior, he will receive a reward. Conversely, an incorrect behavior will result in a correction every time. Let's look at a couple of examples of reinforcement:

1. You are in the kitchen and you see your dog jumping up on the counter to steal a piece of chicken you prepared for tonight's dinner. If you ignore this, then the dog self-reinforces his behavior by getting the chicken. In the dog's mind, this counter is a very positive place to go to, and he will most certainly look up on the counter again in hopes of another great find.

2. In an alternative scenario, you are in the kitchen preparing dinner, and in an attempt to negatively reinforce his behavior, you have placed a distasteful bit of food on the counter (for example, horseradish on a cracker). You leave the room for a minute with only this cracker on the counter, knowing he will take it. When you return he is noticeably uncomfortable with the cracker he just stole. Will he be less likely to jump up on the counter tomorrow? Perhaps, but surely the great chicken meal he once won from the counter will still make him interested in the same spot again. You must continue to provide negative reinforcement setups routinely until the grand kitchen heist is no longer a pleasant memory. He will eventually stop searching your counters if you are consistent with your messages.

You must show your dog, with absolute consistency, what is correct and what is incorrect. All training should be initiated with consistent reinforcement but eventually it should develop into intermittent reinforcement. As your dog becomes more responsible, we can begin to shape and string together new patterns of appropriate behaviors.

When is positive reinforcement used? When is negative reinforcement used? Simply, if you like the behavior your dog is showing, then name the behavior and reward it (positive reinforcement). If your dog shows you an unwarranted behavior then correct it (negative reinforcement), and then only praise your dog after he has demonstrated proper behavior. (I will look a little more closely at the difference between positive reinforcement and negative reinforcement later in the chapter.)

At what point do we begin using intermittent reinforcement? The answer is when your dog clearly understands what is being asked of him and responds quickly with enthusiasm. How intermittently should the reinforcer be used? The answer is that an intermittent reinforcement schedule should be arranged to initially provide an adequate number of rewards per behavior. Ultimately, the reinforcer is only occasionally used for motivation. As the joke goes: if you do fifty recalls with an Afghan hound using food, and on the fifty-first recall you fail to provide a treat, on the fifty-second recall, there will be no dog in sight. The point is that every dog needs its own level of reinforcement. This is something each owner needs to be clear on. Typically, when an owner sees that a particular behavior appears to be mastered, they will then begin trying to get two repetitions or two different behaviors per one food reward. This is how an owner begins to develop an intermittent reinforcement schedule. Shaping occurs as we deprive a reward until we see the second behavior pattern beginning to appear.

There is no shame in giving a reward to a dog for a job well done. Conversely, it is common for me to see owners simply forgetting to provide a positive response, as if it is understood that this correct response is a given. There are very few givens in dog training. Praise in some form must always be given to insure that the dog understands when his response is correct.

One Day's Work for One Day's Pay

Let's take a few minutes and run down the list of what might be considered an appropriate reward. Many people feel that giving food treats is inappropriate. I am here to tell you if the dog likes treats, there is nothing wrong with using them. Most other animals are trained using strictly positive reinforcement. Picture Namu the whale being dragged around a pool by a collar. Pretty ridiculous, huh? It seems that in the United States we are told by many pet professionals that we should never give human food to our dogs because it is unhealthy and unbalanced for them. It may not be balanced but surely it can't be unhealthy. We eat it, and I'm still here to talk about it. Treats for training have to be special. Very special. It is unreasonable to think that we can use a biscuit as a reward if our dog routinely gets them as snacks. If your employer mailed you a check every day for $200 and you didn't have to go into work to earn it, and then suddenly called one day and asked you to come in to work, you might logically ask, "How much money will I get for coming in to work?" If the employer's answer is $200, I believe the next logical question might be, "Will you send the money if I don't come in?" If the boss's response is yes, then you are probably going shopping instead of heading to work. If you give your dog several biscuits a day because you love him, can a biscuit really be considered a special reward for a job well done? I think not. Getting back to the reasons most people fight the treat issue, I have heard the following: my dog will become spoiled and not eat his normal dog food, my dog will beg at the table or begin stealing scraps from the table, my dog will only respond to my commands in the presence of food if I reward him with food, my dog will get sick if I give him people food.

I have heard from many Europeans that we Americans are unkind because we feed our carnivore friends cereal instead of meat. It is a good point to mention how dogs are invited into restaurants in Europe and tend to be very well behaved. In the United States, dogs are rarely allowed in eateries, most likeky because they just don't understand the rules, so the health department says "no dogs allowed." Feeding a dog for training does not mean there is no discipline. I am only stating what much of the world already knows. People food should not make a normal dog sick. Begging or stealing food and other bad behavior does not stem from giving human food as treats. Bad behaviors are the result of not teaching the correct responses in the first place and oftentimes we inadvertently reinforce them. Jumping is just one common example. It seems that many of us think that it's okay to allow jumping on a specific person or just sometimes. Logically, we know we are being unfair, but functionally we deny it and continually reinforce the jumping behavior with smiles and strokes when there are dirty paws on our legs, waist, or chest. If we don't want our dogs jumping sometimes, then we can't let them jump up any time.

Corrections

Many dog trainers today feel that correcting your dog is not necessary. They will tell you that in the absence of a reward, most bad behaviors extinguish themselves. I disagree with this concept only because, in my own experience, I have seen dogs not only continue their bad behaviors but actually escalate these inappropriate behaviors to the point where it has become very difficult to correct them. Behaviors such as barking can be self-reinforcing. Therefore, the dog positively reinforces himself with barking. Extinction of the barking is unlikely without negative reinforcement.

I had a case where a large one-year-old male rottweiler had become aggressive toward strangers. My advice was to have the owners deprive the dog of attention, affection, and food. The point of this deprivation was to have the dog needy enough to allow his fulfillment to come from the arrival of strangers. There was also some conditioning at the doorway to teach the dog to remain calm at the sound of a knock and a ring of the bell. When the stranger arrived, we had the dog sit quietly at the doorway. The stranger was then asked to throw special food treats toward the very hungry dog. As the dog appeared to be very positively interested in the great treat, we asked the stranger to slowly move closer toward the dog, all the while feeding him. The dog appeared to be excited by the treats and was soon taking the treats from the stranger's hand with no sign of aggression.

Sound good? Well, after several weeks of conditioning, using different strangers and a variety of special food treats, it seemed to be working. Later, the dog began to take the treat and then try to bite the bearer of the food. This clearly was not the point of all this work. The goal was to teach the rottweiler to enjoy the arrival of strangers and remain friendly. This conditioning was not working in the way it was meant to. We added corrections to the plan. We continued the positive reinforcement from the outsiders using food treats, but when the dog started to growl or lunge toward the visitor, the owner was instructed to give the dog a strong leash and collar correction. These actions showed the dog how strongly the owner objected to his aggressive behavior. Over the next couple of weeks, the dog began looking at his owner for direction in the presence of strangers. I needed the dog to understand two things: (1) strangers are nice and they bring very good things with them; (2) if I react in an aggressive manner, I am wrong and will be negatively impressed by my owner until I show a friendly and correct response to the visitor. This type of training clearly showed the dog where he must be behaviorally, allowing no chance for confusion. The plan worked.

My point here is that both positive and negative reinforcements are necessary tools in dog training.

Steve's Three Rules

1. Do not use the word No for everything the dog does wrong. How can everything mean "no"? If your dog relieves itself on the floor and you say "no," or the dog jumps on the counter and you say "no," and then your dog barks and you say "no," what does "no" mean? Which of the above does "no" mean? Does "no" mean don't eliminate? Does "no" mean don't jump? Does "no" mean don't bark?

Instead we can say "bad dog" for the elimination problem. We can say "off" for the inappropriate jumping issue. We can say "quiet" for the barking, thus teaching your dog specific terms relating to his behavior.

2. Do not use the dog's name against it, as your parents used your name against you when you were doing something wrong. One day you will call your dog's name to come to you and he will not obey because he will be uncertain whether you are calling his name in a positive or negative manner. You must only use his name in a positive manner.

3. Do not put your pointer finger in your dog's face as a reprimand. If you use the one finger as a hand signal, use it for just one command. You cannot use one signal for a multitude of commands. You will make your dog crazy.

Here are several sample terms you can use to create an appropriate training vocabulary:

Ready	**look at me**
Sit	**to sit**
Stay	**do not move**
Down	**lay down**
Heel	**to left side of handler and sit**
Come	**to front of handler and sit**
Let's go	**same direction together**
Leave it	**do not take in mouth**
Drop	**out of mouth**
Wait	**in a general area**
Off	**no jumping up**
Quiet	**stop barking**
Okay	**release from all commands**
Ouch	**let go of my hand**
Hurry up	**eliminate on command**
Kennel up	**go to crate**

You need to have a plan or an idea of what you want from your dog. If you clearly see the images, show him the pictures he needs to learn in order to please you. Imagine receiving a one-thousand-piece jigsaw puzzle jumbled up in a brown paper bag. You dump it on the floor and immediately know the task of putting it together is going to take a long time. If you were handed a jigsaw puzzle in a box with a picture on the cover you might have a fighting chance, as you refer back to the picture over and over again. It is very important that you become goal-oriented in order to have the best dog he can be. Set attainable goals and go from success to success. Dogs like the feeling of success as much as people do. Once your focus-training has been established, you may begin teaching your dog anything you want.

Eventually, bringing distractions into your training regimen is absolutely necessary in order to teach your dog that he must respond to a command no matter what else is going on at any given moment. Once your dog has learned to focus you may begin adding new locations to the process, in addition to physical distractions. A truly well-trained dog is capable of tuning out these distractions and can respond correctly in the midst of them. Teaching dogs, though, requires your time and commitment.

The Key Elements to Successful Dog Training

Balance

Learning how to balance positive and negative reinforcement in order to achieve the best results is one of the essential keys to successful training. I would love to say that positive reinforcement is all that's needed to insure a well-behaved dog, but my experience shows that a certain degree of negative reinforcement is crucial to help the dog understand that there are unpleasant consequences to bad behavior.

What is bad behavior? Does whatever we consider inappropriate constitute bad behavior? Remember that, above all, we must not create conflict with the very animal that we are trying to build a relationship with and if your dog is attempting to fulfill his instincts and you interfere, there will be conflict. It is your job to help your dog to fulfill his drives in an appropriate way. After all, you are in the same pack, and your dog expects your support. You cannot have the dog shut down his drives, but you can help channel them to be more correct for all concerned.

An example of this may be when a hunting dog chases a rabbit in your yard. You would rather the dog not chase rabbits, so rather than correcting the chase behavior, redirect it to a more suitable target—a favorite toy, a round of Frisbee, or a long game of fetch. Will this new game help extinguish the old "chase the bunny game" completely? Probably not, but with the help of a little negative reinforcement, you and your dog might find some common ground you can both live with.

Timing

Great training requires great timing. Timing is one of the most essential tools in dog training. Your good timing helps the misbehaving dog realize when he is wrong. It is the "incorrect behaviors" that need fixing, not the dog. Timing helps the dog understand this concept. Several times a week, I receive calls from clients who have punished their dog's bad behavior "after the fact." People do not mean to be harsh, yet they feel compelled to punish any wrongdoings that have occurred while they were out shopping for dog food. Coming in and punishing your dog long after the crime has been committed is wrong. He will be afraid but not be learning how to avoid the unwanted behavior again. Timing of corrections is critical in order for your dog to truly understand the nature of his wrongdoing.

I receive many phone calls from well-meaning owners who try to convince me that their dogs know that they did something wrong while the owners were away at work. They come home to some kind of mess, and when they open the door, the dog has a "guilty" look on its face. My take on "the look" is that the owners have shown the dog the mess after the fact often enough so that the association of the mess is clear. The problem is that the dog does not recall making this mess. A dog's memory is often short term. Within only minutes, dogs have forgotten previous events. Therefore, when you walk into your home and you show the dog the mess, he clearly realizes that he is in trouble. He just has no recollection of his part in making the mess. If you cannot connect the actual event to the mess, your dog will not stop making trouble in your absence. It really doesn't make any sense to point out a mess on the floor to your dog because you are only teaching him to worry about messes on the floor and not teaching him how not to make a mess in the first place. This must be done while he is in the act of making the mess.

Timing is equally relevant when rewarding a dog for good behavior. Any significant lapse of time deems a reward wasted. Rewards must be given as the good behavior is exhibited.

Remote Punishment

Remote punishment aids in the learning process so that your dog understands he is clearly being punished by virtue of his own behavior. As your dog learns the negative consequence of his own inappropriate behavior, your dog will become more responsible.

If your dog jumps up and takes a dish towel hanging off a rack and chews it, then he has fulfilled his desire for chewing. If you catch him in the act and correct him by saying "leave it" and then give him an acceptable toy, then you have "walked the walk" for your dog. He must eventually "walk the walk" to the correct toy by himself. Encourage the dog to play with his toy, but do not hand it to him. You can try kicking a toy with your foot and let the dog chase it.

Remote punishment helps the dog to learn these things for himself. If you were to leave several empty soda cans on top of the towel and your dog went to pull the towel down, the cans would fall on him, maybe startling him enough not to try this behavior again. You were not involved in this event, therefore there is no conflict between you and your dog, the conflict is with taking the towel off the bar. When owners correct dogs for these behaviors, at best their dogs are well behaved only in the presence of the owner, and not well behaved in the absence of their owner. Remote punishment teaches responsibility.

Fulfillment

It is very important that your dog's toys be interesting enough for the dog to want them more than anything else around. Start by taking inappropriate items away and providing toys that intensely stimulate your dog's senses and desires. There are various toys on the market that are safe to chew. Hollow toys can be filled with one or more of your dog's favorite treats. Why would a dog chew a shoe when there is food falling out of a toy?

Understanding the needs of your dog will help you to avoid

incorrect behavior in the future. When an owner does not provide an opportunity for a puppy to explore his environment the very first time the leash is taken off, he will run away. Dogs must fulfill their drive to investigate their territory. If you do not allow for this in a controlled way, the dog will struggle to fulfill itself in any manner that works, including running away the very first chance it gets. Play drive is very strong in most dogs, therefore it is important to fulfill that desire. Again, if you do not play with your dog enough, he will look for someone who will play with him.

Basic training is often connected to play drive in order to help your dog enjoy his positive response to your commands. It is the wise dog owner who uses the dog's drives and traits in the best interest of his training. Teaching your dog requires him to initially respond to your command in order to fulfill his urges and desires.

Patience

You must have infinite patience while teaching your dog. It is imperative that you not become angry when things aren't going your way. Getting mad and yelling will certainly scare him, but he will not learn anything except fear. Remember to always give your dog the benefit of the doubt. If you think he may have forgotten or did not hear a command, or was not completely focused, show him again what you want from him.

Canine Responsibility

Let's take a minute to discuss what dog trainers call "area of influence." This term is used to describe the control that one has or does not have at a given distance be it while you are in sight or when you are out of the house.

It is very common to see an owner reach for his dog's collar and see the dog avoid the grasp by quickly jumping back. This game of keep away is the last thing in the world you want your dog to learn. It takes a dog very few repetitions to learn how to be—what he considers—successful for himself.

In order to teach your dog that a correct response is required regardless of the distance you are from him, you must be able to reinforce the command that you made. A simple word from you is not enough, and you must employ physical reinforcement.

Try negative reinforcement by using a long line to maintain "area of influence" and effect his behavior by insuring a correct response. If your dog fails to come when called, a sharp yank on the long line will remind him that you can touch him from anywhere.

Then, help him recover from the correction by using an edible reinforcer or a favorite toy to reward the dog for his correct response. While it is not always the best choice, it tends to lend itself to wide use, because of the apparent lack of physical force.

If you ever intend to leave your dog out of the crate while you are out of the house, your dog must show you some level of responsibility. Begin leaving your dog out of his confined space for short periods while you are somewhere in your home and capable of correcting any misbehaviors. Any wrongdoing should be corrected by taking hold of your dog's house lead and making a timely correction. After the correction, you both go back to doing whatever you were doing before. Do not talk about misbehavior. Correct it and move on. I prefer that you don't crate your dog after an incident that has been corrected. If necessary, help your dog find a project like chewing a toy or doing a short "down-stay." Crate use should be limited to a time when you cannot monitor your dog's behavior. Giving your dog something to do after he has been corrected will help prevent another negative occurrence. It is far better to have your dog be free of the crate and be well behaved as this is the long-term goal.

When your dog is totally reliable in your presence then you can begin to leave him alone for very brief periods. Extend the free time slowly, and as long as your dog remains correct, continue to prolong his free time while you are out. The first time you have a relapse, go back and reduce his time and build his time back up slowly. Your dog needs to be responsible while you are away, and although crates are convenient, adult dogs should be capable of a successful "run of the house." Take your time. Don't get lazy. Keep the training up and get Fido out of his crate. It's best for all concerned.

Your teaching method will be dictated by the character of your dog. Let's remember that when teaching our friends, the components to keep in mind are:

1. Teach, don't correct.

2. Show your dog a clear picture of what you want from him.

3. Determine what this dog can give us as an individual.

4. Determine what commitment, in terms of training, you are willing to make to get what you want.

Above all, have patience with your dog, because if you are a good teacher, he will be a good student. Always blame yourself for any failure relating to the teaching process. Do not blame your dog.

5.

....

Common
Behavioral
Problems

Anything that an animal does is considered behavior. The most basic of motions, the blink of an eye, a turn of the head, or even a simple inhalation, are all behaviors. It is common to overlook the motivations of any given motion, but you must learn to recognize what triggers your dog's responses to any given stimulus to successfully train your animal.

Based on many of the telephone calls that I receive from owners, a significant number ask for obedience classes to correct a behavioral problem, but obedience training is not always the solution to these problems.

Most of the time, your dog is just being himself for better or for worse. If he is phobic about something in his environment then you will see his phobia become manifested through his behavior. He may hide or become agitated when triggered by whatever it is that scares

him. These behaviors may or may not be a problem for your dog, yet they will always be a problem for you. If you are having aggression problems with your dog, it is possible that your dog is gaining the upper hand. This is not so great for you and not so bad for your dog. If your dog is fearful, then both you and your dog have a problem. As a responsible owner, you should do whatever you can to help resolve your dog's fears.

These behavioral problems sometimes present themselves despite the good care and training that you have provided. There are individuals in prisons who are highly intelligent and have graduated from Ivy League schools at the top of their classes. They are bad guys who are smart, but they are bad. Dogs are often this way. Smart and bad. I love the old "There are no bad dogs in the world" theory. This is the most ridiculous thing I've ever heard. There are many bad dogs in this world. Often it is the fault of breeders and irresponsible owners. But sometimes it is simply the weak character of the individual dog.

Dogs possess inherent behaviors, so when you purchase a rottweiler, you'd better not think he will have the temperament of a golden retriever. Dogs also have emotions, and they cannot be emotionally hostile and friendly simultaneously. These emotional states constantly fluctuate along with the drives of your dog. When attempting to change your dog's behavior, you must be well versed in various approaches.

Although we have discussed behavioral theory, it is often a bit difficult to apply esoteric solutions to your dog's problems. The following are difficult situations encountered by dog owners as well as realistic solutions to the problems.

Aggression

The most common behavioral problem encountered in my practice is aggression, of which there are many categories. They have been classified and defined by various veterinary and Ph.D. behaviorists in the United States and Europe over the last decade or so.

Dominance Aggression

Dominance aggression is centered toward one or more family members. Dominance may be an inherent urge to rise to the top of the pecking order or it may be a learned response. Acts of dominance aggression may be hormonally induced. Dominance aggression usually appears between the ages of one and three years and is seen predominantly in male dogs. This does not mean that it cannot occur in younger or older dogs, nor does it mean that this type of aggression is never seen in females.

I have had success in retraining dogs who showed dominant behavior as a result of inadvertent reinforcement by the owner. I have had cases where if the dog was on the owner's bed, the owner had to sleep on the couch. This situation came about from the dog growling to protect the bed and the owner allowing the dog to keep the position. Oftentimes, simply having better control of the dog by using a house lead to physically remove him if he growls helps to reduce the overall aggression.

Although dominant behavior can be exhibited by any breed or mixed breed, there are a few breeds of dog that are said to be dominant breeds. Rottweilers, Akitas, German shepherd dogs, chow chows, and Lhasa Apsos are among them. I have seen many male dogs become passive after surgical neutering but interestingly, I have seen several cases of dominant behavior appear only *after* the neutering.

When dominance is an inherent characteristic of your dog's behavior, then the aggression may be managed but not eradicated. Dogs that are inherently dominant will chronically challenge authority. Recognizing the dominance is the first step to its management. Management can be quite effective when the dog owner is willing to change some of his own behaviors in an effort to change his dog's aggressive behavior.

Behavioral Sketch of a Dominant Aggressive Dog

History. An unneutered three-year-old Lhasa Apso male was obtained by a family with two young girls, ages ten and fourteen, when he was eight weeks old. The family purchased the puppy from a private hobby breeder with a good reputation.

The dog did well in puppy kindergarten and basic obedience classes. He was well cared for in terms of medical and nutritional requirements, and he was adequately exercised.

Aggressive events. The dog showed aggression toward the adult woman of the house when she tried to brush him. Although he had been brushed an endless number of times, he suddenly tried to bite her one day. Logically, the woman thought that she may have somehow hurt him or maybe he had a knot in his coat or an inflamed insect bite. Although the dog ran away from her, she pursued him so that she could examine him and make sure he was okay. The dog would not come to her, and when she tried to reach toward him, he growled and lunged forward. The owner saw that the dog was upset and left him alone for a while. Even though she saw a look of remorse on his face, he appeared withdrawn. Later he was fine, and she was able to treat her dog as usual. He even tolerated brushing with no problem again. Three days later, he was under the living room coffee table when his owner called him to "come" so he could go for his final evening walk. He failed to come out, and when his owner got on her knees and reached under the table the dog growled and lunged at her. She then jiggled his leash in an attempt to excite him about his walk but received no response. She really wanted to get the walk over with and go to bed herself, but he would just not come out. Finally she began to get firm with him and raised her voice so the dog knew she wasn't kidding around. This only resulted in a louder growl from the dog. The louder the owner yelled, the louder the dog growled. Each time she reached out toward him, he lunged at her with his lips retracted and his teeth bared. She went off to bed saying, "Forget this, let him suffer with a full bladder." When she woke up in the morning, she found her dog at the foot of the bed where he always slept. When the dog awoke, he was his usual bright and normal self. He had even avoided elimination accidents over the course of the night.

In this sample profile of dominance, this dog failed to show aggression to anyone else in this family. He only exerted his dominance over his primary caregiver, the one who gave him the most time, love, and energy.

Dominance aggression is a very common form of aggression because of its inherent nature. In order for the human owner to achieve and maintain dominance, he must understand the dog's urges and know how to diffuse them in a positive manner. It is important to note that dominant dogs generally escalate their aggression when physical corrections are administered via leash and collar.

Overwhelming physical force has backed many of these dogs down yet often proved to be only a temporary solution. Again, the drive assessment helps to determine how hard or easy it will be to live with this type of dog.

Treatment plan. Management generally consists of learning how not to trigger aggressive responses. If you call your dog and he will not come, leave him alone. If you want to pet him and you call him over with success, you may pet him; otherwise, do not go to him. Praise him only when he responds to your command to come. Do not go to him and stroke him when he will not come to you. Furthermore, remember not to pet him when he comes over, nudging you with his nose, pushing at your arm for some strokes. It is important that you don't acknowledge demanding behavior in order not to encourage these demanding tendencies. The common areas to recognize and control the hierarchical structure include:

Who sleeps in the best spot. The best spot is that area that is considered either most comfortable or closest to the dominant figure in the pack.

Who eats first. Survival of the fittest insures that the strong eat before anyone else. Feed yourself first.

Who walks in front. He who is in front is the leader. If you are always following your dog, he is the leader and you are the follower. Commonly, dogs are walked on a lead, and they pull their owners constantly around the neighborhood. Why would the dog think that the owner is in charge? When your dog passes in front of you, turn and walk in the opposite direction. Now you are in front.

Who protects the pack. The strong protect the pack. When your dog has a hard time settling down when a visitor arrives at your door, and the barking appears to be somewhat aggressive, the dog assumes that it is his job to inspect and decide who can and who cannot enter his domain. This may be a manifestation of a protection or dominant drive. It is up to you to teach your dog that he is not to be involved in protection issues because you will take care of such problems for him.

Who owns the toys. The dog that can control his toys may be inadvertently trained to guard his toys. Leaving his toys around for him to play with at his will may suggest ownership of these toys. It is a good habit to take your dog's toys away when he is not using them and give them to him when you wish to play.

Who controls the play time. Dogs will almost throw their toys or balls in your lap in an attempt to elicit play from you. Although this can be a harmless act, it may also be a dominant act as well. Be sure to initiate play on your terms; it is amazing what a dog will do for his owner for a short play session. Use play as a reward for your dog's compliant behavior.

Who controls caregiving. The dominant members care for the subordinate members. The dominant may allow others to provide care, but it is always on their terms. Should an omega member of the structure take it upon himself to provide care, without permission from the alpha member, a fight may ensue.

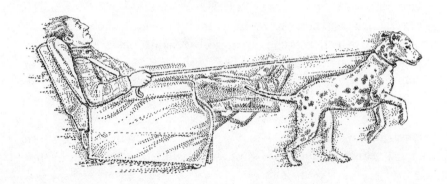

Social Aggression/Dominance Status

These terms are associated with the aggression that dogs show to one another in an attempt to claim and maintain hierarchical peace.

Some dogs are aggressive because they lack social experience, while others have had traumatic past experiences, such as having been attacked by a larger and older dog when they were puppies. Most often the aggressive events tend to appear to center around a status issue.

Territorial Aggression

This frequent form of aggression is considered normal in many breeds because it is natural to protect the territory in which the pack lives. Several working breeds were specifically bred to have this as a pronounced instinct.

Drive down to your local junkyard and you will surely find dogs barking behind a fence, looking very ferocious. You will feel certain that if they should escape, your life would come to an end. Many of these dogs are showing the effects of boundary frustration, as well as territorial aggression. Dogs that are contained to a property via tie-out cables, kennel runs, or fences frequently show the effects of boundary frustration. The inability to socially interact with those on the "other side" creates suspicion often resulting in aggression.

Aggressive events. I have been in homes where the dog would let me enter the home without barking too much but would fiercely attack me if I tried to leave the house or even bend over in my chair. Once, a female German shepherd came after me when I barely moved to reach into my attaché case for a pen. I have a friend who works for UPS, and he always tells me stories about his dog experiences while out delivering packages to homes and businesses. According to Nick you just need to know that the dog is there and he feels that it's his job to protect his property. The next step is being able to evaluate whether you have an all-bark situation or the real deal coming at you like a freight train with every intention of tasting blood.

Many dogs that are barking behind a fence will not bite should they escape the yard. They will just run off with their newfound freedom, only to return later when they are feeling fulfilled and a little hungry. However, there are dogs who will not only bite the first stranger in sight, but will kind of "do the neighborhood" threatening and/or biting anyone in their path.

Treatment plan. The behavioral prognosis for territorial aggression is guarded. The dog who shows this behavior must quickly become aware that the aggression is unacceptable to you, the owner. Usually, this is done by employing conventional leash and collar corrections. The problem with using simple negative reinforcement is that this does not address the state of the dog. The state we are talking about is hostility. Correcting the dog will not change the dog from hostile to friendly, although it may result in compliance at best. What would be in everyone's best interest is to have the dog actually enjoy the approach of strangers, which makes the behavior much more secure. The good behavior does not then rely on the presence of the owner.

In order to achieve this, the dog might need to be kenneled away from the home for about a week. This helps to displace the territorial behavior. Upon coming home the dog is then frequently moved about from one room to another, with the owner being clearly in control of where the dog is allowed to be. Imagine that every time your dog is confined to a room where he can see the mailman coming to deliver the mail, he barks at him until he leaves to deliver your neighbor's mail. In your dog's mind, your dog has scared the intruder away. This makes your dog feel strong and reinforces his ability to successfully protect his territory.

When territorial aggression is a problem, do not allow your dog to feel it "owns" your property. If you are clear on the behavior that is acceptable here, then your dog will be clear too. If you want to give your dog the responsibility of guarding your home, then I hope you have good liability insurance. I feel that as long as I pay the mortgage, then it is up to me who may come and go around my house. I personally don't even allow barking at the door; I find it scares children, so I teach my dogs to be quiet at the sound of the knock and the bell. Once good doorway behavior is trained prophylactically, then an overall reaction of territorial behavior is generally seen.

If territorial aggression is sought after as a means of protection, the opposite holds true and dogs should be tied out or agitated through a fence with the "loud guy" always running away, making the dog feel successful with its show of aggression. Be aware of training your dog this way. Remember your liability.

Possessive Aggression

Possessive aggression is centered around a dog's food, toys, treats, or any article that the dog may have stolen from you.

Aggressive events. I had a case where the only thing the dog guarded was a real cow femur. Other food and treats could easily be taken from this dog at any time but you were history if you thought you were getting the femur back. He was a large German shepherd dog, but being that he was so super all the rest of the time, the cow femurs were removed from the house. It wasn't difficult to find a new suitable replacement for his chewing needs. Some cases are not so easy. I had a case where a Siberian husky hid a marrow bone under the couch. Maybe it just slid under the couch by accident, but the owner told me the dog had a history of burying and hiding things. One day the owner's nine-year-old son jumped belly first onto the couch. In order to guard his bone, the dog attacked the boy, who had no knowledge that the bone was under the couch. The dog bit the boy several times but the parents were able to restrain the dog. Luckily, after receiving medical attention, the boy was fine. The dog was placed in a home with no children and a well-contained backyard. Then, the dog was fine, too.

Treatment plan. Possessive aggression should not be handled primarily with compulsion (negative reinforcement). It should be handled with positive conditioning.

The scenario: a dog starts to growl when his owner approaches him while chewing his pig's ear. You can correct this behavior when you are prepared to teach the dog to act in a less defensive manner around his pig's ear. The technique requires you to first offer the dog his pig's ear, then walk away. Get out one of your dog's favorite treats, making it the best it can be, so it is much more appealing than the pig's ear. Throw or drop the food directly in front of the dog and walk away. If the dog growls, however, as you approach him, walk away and leave no food. If the dog growled, you went too close to him and you should throw the treat from a distance, so as not to elicit any aggression from the dog. You may decrease the space between you and the dog gradually. This process usually takes several weeks of slowly building the dog's trust so that he understands you are approaching him to give, and not to take away from him. Generally, these sessions should be very short, but frequent. The treat is fabulous, but each repetition should only give the dog a small amount of food so as to keep him interested in learning how to earn greater rewards. Five or six repetitions per session with about four training sessions daily will generally do.

It is wise not to leave anything for the dog to "own" while you are training him. That includes toys, chews, beds, empty food bowls, and pigs' ears. Provide the treats when you are practicing your approach conditioning. We will move along to the point where we drop the treats between his legs or have him directly take the food from your hand. We will proceed to the point where you can take his pig's ear, give him a treat, and then return his pig's ear to him to chew. In this way you can functionally teach your dog to look forward to your approach when he has an object, and if necessary allow you to take the object with no anxiety or aggression from him. This will work only if you follow the program and do it slowly. After you have achieved success, continue this process intermittently forever. It can only be helpful. Also, note that a dog that knows how to drop something out of his mouth on command tends toward less possessive aggression.

It is critical that all members of your family participate in this program in order for the dog to generalize his correct behavior.

Always be aware that this possessive aggression may arise again if an unforeseen incident provokes defensive actions on the part of your dog. Your dog's aggression is an action that occurs in hopes that the target of his aggression will exhibit avoidance behaviors and walk or run away, therefore allowing him to fulfill his defensive drive.

Although I feel strongly about handling this problem through conditioning, I would be criminal in my responsibility as a counselor to omit the possibility of using negative reinforcement if the conditioning fails to work sufficiently. In some cases I have had to set dogs up with objects, knowing full well they would become possessive. To this end, I would attach a long lead to their collars, and when they showed even a little glimpse of aggression, I physically moved them away from the object via the long line and then did strong basic obedience routines for fifteen minutes. Afterward, I would return the object and approach the dog. If there was a growl I would once again pull the dog briskly away from his object and make a strong fifteen-minute session again. Strong doesn't mean angry or loud but fast and physically exhausting.

Generally, this ritual helps the dog to understand your strength and that the consequence of his aggression is going to be hard work—every time. When the dog leaves the object on command he is well rewarded with play, praise, petting, and occasionally food.

Both positive and negative reinforcement can and should be used together.

Protective Aggression

Protective aggression is often associated with dominance aggression because it is the job of the pack leader to protect the pack. Problem is, as with all forms of aggression, there are no hard and fast rules.

History. I received a phone call from a family that owned a spaniel-size female mixed-breed that was about seven years old. They found the dog when she was a two-year-old, tied to a parking meter in New York City. The family consisted of Mom, Dad, and two daughters who had moved out of the city to the suburbs when the girls were five and nine years old. At the time I was called, the family had lived in their home for about two years, and the girls were then about seven and eleven. Both parents still worked in the city and an au pair had been hired to care for the daughters.

Aggressive events. The incident that prompted the call was one of aggression. A visitor arrived at their home, and when the door was opened, the dog jumped at him and ripped his lower lip from his jaw. The dog had never shown aggression of any kind ever before. There was no apparent provocation.

Initially, I didn't want to take the case. I thought that a dog that has the courage to jump all the way up into someone's face and bite should be euthanized. After all, there are children in the family, and they are a priceless treasure. The family insisted that I see the dog, and since the correct thing to do as a trainer was to see her with my own eyes, I made a visit to their home. I knocked and rang the bell. The evening I made my visit, there was not a sound from behind the door. I had asked that the dog be dragging a leash when I arrived so we could have a bit of control should this dog decide she wanted to eat my face too. When the door opened I did not see her. She was not locked away but in another room choosing to stay near the girls, despite the fact that a stranger was visiting.

As the dog came out to greet me, I could see her friendly demeanor. There were no signs of aggression. I asked the family dog-related questions for two hours, including information about her training, health, and all the years of her ownership by this family. Clearly, finding her anonymously tied to a parking meter left us with about two blank years. But in the five years of ownership, all in all she had been a happy, healthy, and above all, friendly and nonaggressive dog. She was excellent with the girls and extremely compliant to commands from every family member, as well as from the au pair.

I finally began to ask questions about the man who had been bitten. No one in this family really liked this man. He went to school with the au pair, and she allowed him to come over for visits, but did not really like him. The mom said he was a nice guy but made the kids hyperactive. The girls said he played a little too roughly with them and even though they liked him, they thought he was a bit too much.

That evening I found a lovely dog at this home. I classified the event as a protective aggressive event. The dog perceived this young man as a potential threat to the girls and made a strong attempt at ridding the family of their problems. Obviously, the family didn't want to see this young man get bitten by their dog, but the dog had acted in good faith from its perspective.

Treatment plan. There are no miracle solutions for this type of problem. It must be clear to your dog that the job of pack protection is in your hands not theirs. If your dog is strong in his instinct to protect, management will be necessary to prevent aggressive events. Routinely showing your dog correct hierarchic structure will generally help to curtail protective aggressive behaviors. Show your dog that you are the leader and if necessary will protect him in an emergency. Routine obedience exercises often help an owner to reinforce deference in their dog.

Competitive Aggression

Competitive aggression is often seen in homes where the dog was treated like a baby until your first newborn arrives.

It is common for dog owners to be a bit anxious when bringing a new baby into the home. The chaos of this joyous event throws your dog "off" a little. (I'll discuss this unique situation a little more in chapter 7.)

Fear-Related Aggression

Fear lives in the hearts of many dogs. A dog that is fearful may bite simply to discourage you, or whatever is threatening him, to go away. Dogs often prefer to threaten with vocal and physical displays, but when they feel backed up against the wall, they will bite.

Dogs biting out of fear generally bite fast and hard, but they usually release the grip quickly. They may rebite if they are not yet fulfilled, meaning you may still be stimulating aggression by screaming or swatting at the dog. Any type of fighting from you may only increase the overall time of the incident. The dog will only be fulfilled when it produces avoidance from you or whomever the event is focused toward. These types of dogs are generally nervous and for the most part naturally display active defense drives.

The prognosis on this type of aggression depends on the actual nerve threshold of the dog and the skill of the owner. A well-schooled handler can recognize apprehension on the dog's part and ward off an incident before it begins. Learning to read your dog comes with time and experience.

I have had fairly good success treating nervous dogs, using both positive and negative reinforcement with modality (behavioral technique), depending on the individual case. I cannot offer any general advice in this area of fear-related aggression, other than to be aware of the dog's emotions at all times. As strange as it may sound, I have helped nervous dogs calm down with leash and collar corrections. Dogs are sometimes nervous because they are uncertain of their environment and stature. Leash correction on this type of nervousness resolves the dog's conflict. It creates a structure with definite organization. When pushing nerve thresholds back, care must be taken to recognize how much nerve quality is gained so as to prevent accidental bites. Owners of such dogs are responsible for trying to resolve the fear by exposing the dog in a safe way to various experiences. These cases should be handled by skilled professionals.

Pain-Induced Aggression

This type of aggression is considered to be somewhat normal. When I was a child, I once kicked my dentist in the chest with my foot and sent him flying across the room when he began drilling in my mouth. I think we can safely call my reaction to the drilling pain-induced aggression. Fear of pain may also incite an aggressive response. A good owner should understand that under some circumstances, even the best of dogs might react with aggression. I have worked with dogs who after receiving cervical (neck) disc discomfort showed aggression when their owner tried to put their collar on so that they could go for a walk. The dog's fear of pain created the aggressive reaction. Counterconditioning was extremely helpful in resolving this case. Initially the sight of the collar equaled food, then bringing the collar near the dog's head equaled food. Ultimately, the collar was placed on the dog, the dog was rewarded, and the collar was removed.

The dog was carefully walked on a body harness until the disc problem was resolved, as to prevent any further pain connected with a collar. The collar ultimately equaled food and soon the dog looked forward to the collar being placed on. Although the dog was controlled, he also wore his collar while being walked, so that he would see the collar as a positive tool.

Maternal Aggression

Many normally friendly female dogs become aggressive when they are nursing a litter of puppies. It is important to be very careful about letting visitors around the mother while she is tending to her puppies. Some bitches will show aggression even toward their owners at this time.

Generally this aggression passes as the puppies grow older, and the bitch becomes less protective over them.

Should you encounter this problem, wait until the bitch needs to go out for a walk or feed her in a room away from the puppies. In this way, you can examine the puppies and make sure that they all appear healthy.

Intermale Aggression

Male dogs will frequently fight. Even brothers (littermates) will fight after they mature, though they have been raised together. I have seen fights between a big dog and a little dog that ended in the death of the little dog.

Intact (unneutered) males tend to fight more often than castrated males, although I have seen males that were friendly toward dogs until shortly after the castration, at which time they became very aggressive toward dogs. I can only speculate as to why this might happen. Perhaps the dog was clear in his drives prior to the surgical castration, and as his hormone level drops, he becomes somewhat confused as to how to behave around other male dogs. It may be that he becomes fearful of being attacked or his mechanism for defensive behavior is overstimulated.

I have solved this problem by having the two offending males wear basket muzzles and allowing them to fight, with no chance of either getting hurt. This technique is only viable if the two dogs are of similar size, otherwise the larger dog may still hurt the smaller one. It is important to monitor the dogs when using this procedure. I have also had two males of similar size heavily tranquilized when I was worried that even with the muzzles there might be harm done. Sometimes I have had owners keep their dogs medicated for several weeks in an attempt to allow time for the hierarchy to be established.

Often, it is a dog's hormonal activity that produces a dominance status issue, producing the trigger to fight, and if this seems to be the case surgical castration is generally a sound recommendation.

Interfemale Aggression

Although it is more common to find aggression among males, females have been known to fight with great ferocity. Fights tend to be more common during estrus (heat) because of increased hormone levels. As there is a dominant male to each litter, there is a dominant female as well. The loudest female is thought to be the most dominant female—a good tip to take along with you when looking at a litter of puppies.

Redirected Aggression

Redirected aggression is aggression focused toward a benign subject or object. Dogs may displace their aggression on to other dogs or people when they are in pain or in a frantic state. In some attempt for fulfillment, a dog will just bite whatever or whoever is near them.

I have also seen a dog turn around and bite the other dog in the family while receiving electronic corrections during training for boundary containment. Perhaps this dog believed it was bitten by the other dog first. I have seen dogs bite their handlers when given strong leash corrections. Dogs that bite quickly in this reactive manner must be carefully handled. Many dogs are sound in their overall temperament yet will display redirected aggression if overstimulated.

Frequently train these dogs, using focus exercises. One benefit of gaining focus from your dog is to temporarily distract your dog, thus preventing hectic behaviors.

Aggression Displays After Spaying and Neutering

Behavioral effects aside, unless you are going to breed, show, or work your dog, it should be spayed or neutered. There are numerous health benefits in favor of these procedures, and while it is far from natural to sterilize animals, we must be responsible for their overpopulation and poor breeding practices.

Behaviorally speaking, male dogs may become less aggressive overall in their territorial and pack behaviors. Leg-lifting behavior may not develop in a dog that is neutered prepubertally. Also, becuse of its hormonal influence on territorial behavior, inappropriate indoor leg lifting often disappears after neutering. In addition, I have witnessed a decline in roaming behavior and postneuter mounting tendencies as well.

I have seen a few problems trying to train dogs for protection after they had been neutered but have also had an equal number of successes. It is my opinion that a working dog should be hormonally intact. Hardness has its benefits in correct situations, and that is an important concept for everybody to remember. Many people get testy should they notice testicles hanging off your dog, but anyone who can control their intact male dog deserves to have him that way. Remember though that his health will eventually dictate whether to have the procedure or not.

With bitches, estrogen is no longer produced after the spay, and therefore it is possible for a female to appear more malelike in her behaviors. These behaviors may include dog fighting, territorial protection, and frequent territorial urination often accompanied by leg lifting.

Although I strongly feel that you should adhere to your veterinarian's recommendations, I personally like to have dogs intact until they are almost fully grown. Statistically one can argue that the best behavioral benefits occur from early castration in male dogs. I think having the procedure done early may prevent the onset of territorial leg lifting but will not affect dominance behaviors not yet related to hormonal influence. Note that early castration may be a good idea in pet males who show aggressive behaviors as puppies just to prevent any further development of testosterone. I have seen some very aggressive dogs that were neutered, so you must realize that this procedure is not a miracle cure for every inappropriate behavior, because it is not. Dogs that are problematic should be neutered if for no other reason than they should not be bred.

Aggression in dogs is not uncommon. Once faced with the fact that your dog has shown aggressive tendencies, a general sense of fear sets in. You begin to wonder if your dog will really bite you, or in the case that he has already bitten you, will he bite again? As the owner of an aggressive dog, it is your responsibility to make sure public safety is maintained. I have found that in the majority of my aggression cases, owners have failed to manage their dogs carefully enough to be successful. I am certain that every owner made an honest attempt to do the best they could, but aggression can be very difficult to manage. The job of training and managing this type of dog really belongs in the hands of a seasoned professional.

Destructive Behaviors

Chewing

Although chewing is normal behavior for dogs to exhibit, it is not acceptable for them to be chewing our furniture, shoes, stuffed animals, and remote controls. I receive numerous telephone calls from clients whose dogs seem to do nothing but . . . chew!

Why Do Dogs Chew? Chewing may be caused by a variety of stimuli. Puppies frequently chew because of teething discomfort or as part of their normal investigatory behavior. Adult dogs may chew because of boredom or separation anxiety. Dogs often chew as part of their play ritual, or because an item may be palatable and taste good. Sometimes, like any bad behavior, it is simply a bad habit.

Teething. Teething is the normal behavior associated with the loss of a puppy's deciduous (temporary) baby teeth and the appearance of the adult teeth. Human babies are painstakingly cared for during this stage of primary tooth eruption. Parents can be seen in supermarkets at all hours of the day and night looking for saline teething rings to freeze in an attempt to alleviate the discomfort their child is suffering. There are also commercial products on the market to rub onto the child's gums to topically numb the area. But there are no such products for dogs. I actually have sometimes heard veterinarians giving their clients permission to use these human topical products on their dogs' mouths.

There are hard rubber and plastic toys available for puppies to teethe on, but I have found many of these commercially available items very underwhelming in terms of puppy interest. Some puppy owners find that ice cubes or washcloths tied in a knot and dampened and frozen are useful for alleviating mouth discomfort. I have given puppies frozen bagels to help overcome teething pain. Small-breed puppies may have half of a frozen bagel cut down to an appropriate size. Ice cubes are great except they melt down too fast. The frozen rag may be helpful except that you must take it away so the dog does not ingest any of the material after it thaws. Also I worry about making this cloth/mouth association. Will the dog eat your clothes if he finds them on the floor because you offered him a cloth rag to chew on during his young teething days? Perhaps he will, so be aware that you might be providing mixed signals to your dog. Do allow for a variety of tactile sensations to keep your dog interested, but do not provide so many toys that the dog is confused as to what is his and what is yours.

Mouthing. While in their teething period it is normal for puppies to mouth your hands when they become excitable and playful. While most professionals consider this normal, you will most definitely consider it unacceptable. It hurts. Even when a pup is eight weeks old, the temporary teeth are very sharp. This mouthy behavior should be discouraged, for although it is the norm, and this is how puppies communicate with one another, it is unwise to suggest to your puppy that it is fine to communicate with you this way.

Many dog owners believe that it is a fun idea to rough up their puppy and have it jump at them and bite their hands. When this type of play is stimulated by the unknowledgeable owner, it can cause confusion in the dog's mind. In a situation where the dog needs to bark clearly and threaten a stranger, many of these dogs will jump up and bite their owners instead. If you want to teach a dog to keep you safe in potentially dangerous situations, protection training should only be administered by skilled professionals.

Puppies that are destined to be trained for protection work should not be harshly corrected for normal puppy biting. Strong corrections for mouthy behavior may result in an adult dog that will not bite, even if the situation calls for it. Such puppies should be provided with alternate toys and games that may actually promote biting at items such as towels or rope toys.

Most experts prefer no tug-of-war games, and in fact when they do suggest tug-of-war as a fun game, they want the owner to "win." Working-dog pups should be allowed to "win" the tug-of-war at the end of the game to help them build confidence and lose any inhibitions about biting the rag or towel.

I believe that having total control of the tug-of-war game is far better than not playing it at all. Working dogs learn to "take" and "drop" on command. All dogs should learn this.

Boredom. When your dog is alone and confined to a room in your house or tied to a line outside, he will probably become bored and look for something to do. Since he doesn't have thumbs to twiddle, he'll most certainly use his mouth to help pass the time. Exercise may be the solution to this problem, but be aware that exercise can also create chewing. When your dog is pumped up and active with nowhere else to go, he may displace his energy with chewing behaviors. Some dogs tire with exercise, while others become exuberant. It's best to exercise your dog well every day, but afterward take a little time to wind down together. This way you are providing a direct outlet for your dog's drive and positively reinforcing your relationship. Always provide a super chew toy for him, preferably an edible one. Toys with the ability to hold food inside them are commercially available and handy for focusing busy and orally active dogs. Frozen bagels or pizza dough also help to center a bored dog into appropriate chewing.

Fear. I have had cases where dogs chewed up door frames and windowsills to escape a house during a thunderstorm. One owner called to say that every time her neighbors walked their dog past her home, her own dog went ballistic and chewed the window frame in an attempt to get at the intruding animal. These acts of defensive behavior are causes of destructive chewing.

The dog that is busy looking outside a window may be trained to do another behavior, such as a "down-stay" in the kitchen, while your neighbor walks past your house. First, ask your neighbor to pass your home without her dog so that you can begin your training. You will teach your dog to do a great "down-stay" in the kitchen. You may use treats, but be sure to have a lead on your dog to assure his compliance with your "down-stay" command. The "down-stay" is a position whereby your dog is lying down and not moving. This position, once learned, helps to settle dogs that are unsettled, afraid, or aggressive. In the early stages of teaching your dog something new, make it easy for him to concentrate on the lesson and make it easy for him to be correct and successful. First teach him in a distraction-free environment that is familiar, such as a kitchen. Next, teach him in a less familiar environment, still with no distractions. Once it appears that your dog will follow your command in any distraction-free environment, go back to a familiar location and begin providing distractions until your dog complies with your command in any environment under any type of distraction. Over the course of many sessions, you should find it easier to control your dog's aggression at the window, helping to eliminate the destructive chewing. Commercially available electric mats that offer a mild shock similar to the shock you might get from rubbing your feet on the carpet and touching a metal doorknob may keep your dog away from the window. Ultrasonic motion detectors may also deter your dog from approaching the window by sending a very sharp-pitched tone as a negative reinforcer.

When chewing is secondary to the fear of being alone (separation anxiety), negative reinforcers usually create more problems than they solve. These dogs may stop the chewing behavior but are sure to manifest their fear with another inappropriate behavior, such as chronic barking. Conditioning away the fear of being alone will extinguish the chewing.

Play. I have witnessed dogs playing and seen their exuberance create a displacement to biting and to chewing. Often the dog that displaces his energy toward chewing needs significantly more training and a structured exercise program. If your dog sounds as though he fits this category, then you should teach him to be comfortable in his crate when he is alone. Begin to structure his exercise in such a way that his play drive is fulfilled through a variety of training procedures, such as retrieving or jumping routines. Practice many "down-stays" with him indoors and pair exuberant behavior with the outdoors.

Attention seeking. Dogs that need more attention from their owners will learn how to receive it. Negative attention is often viewed by the dog as positive, because attention is attention, and negative attention is better than none at all.

Barking, stealing, chewing, spinning, and limping are just a few of the types of attention-seeking behaviors that I have seen.

Chewing and other attention-seeking behaviors are best not being addressed in any way. Often they can be eliminated through extinction; that is, if you bring no attention to the behaviors they will disappear over time. And as always be sure that your dog is healthy, well exercised, and well fed.

Palatability. The more palatable something is, the more your dog will want to chew it. Chicken bones are dangerous, yet if your dog finds them he will eat them because they taste good. They are palatable as far as he's concerned. This type of chewing is difficult to eliminate unless you "dog-proof" your home. Dog-proofing your home can be done by removing or picking up anything even remotely interesting to your dog. Television remote controls, electric wires, wooden furniture, leather and canvas shoes, stuffed animals, and children's toys are all favorites of chewing dogs. I have used electronic collars to help dogs learn not to pick up tasty items, but if unsupervised many dogs will return to the chewing behavior.

Habitual chewing (oral fixation). Occasionally, puppies are allowed to chew down the house. Maybe it was okay at the time as long as you were redoing the house or maybe because your pup was only destroying the garage. Perhaps you were working all day when he was young and you felt guilty about leaving him in the crate, so you left him enough freedom to eat the tiles off the floor or chew through the wallboard. Now he is older and still chews anything he can get to. Some dogs are actually compulsive about chewing, and they should be treated medically as well as behaviorally.

Treatment for this type of chewing may consist of allowing the dog to chew, but gradually the chewing target is controlled through training. The extreme case is the dog that may become aggressive when you attempt to stop the chewing behavior. These dogs can usually be controlled with psychotropic medications while being conditioned to be less interested in oral activity or conditioned to choose a specific oral reinforcer. The use of short-term medication is often valuable to the overall solution of a problem. Getting a veterinarian's opinion about your dog's behavioral health is imperative in order to gain the fullest degree of information and help. Puppies chew when they are teething, a phase that lasts until their adult teeth have come in. Usually the adult teeth will have erupted by five months of age, but puppies will sometimes continue to chew for another month or so. Puppies that are chewing a lot after six months of age are doing so for reasons other than teething.

Digging

Digging may be breed related. Terriers have been bred for digging out varmints, while sled dogs dig to create a den where they can sleep. Dogs dig in order to get to mud, which is cooler to lie in than hot sand or topsoil. They dig when they are left alone and isolated, and they dig to hide bones and toys to be retrieved at a later date or not.

Dogs that are given small hard plastic baby pools in the summer seem to dig considerably less than dogs that have no other options for cooling off. Some dogs do well when trained to dig in a specific area only. I like to get the dog out of the yard for a while and keep him close to me for a few weeks so that the habit may pass and I can reinforce all good behaviors, or at least redirect the poor behaviors toward the positive goal. Over time, and initially only in my presence, will the dog have access to the yard. I will slowly increase the time that I will leave the dog alone in the yard and be certain to leave something safe for him to play with or chew.

Worst-case scenario is punishment, which has been effective in treating digging problems. Water hosing the dog from a hidden location when he begins digging will stop the behavior for a while, but for how long? Who knows. I prefer the long drawn-out way. Hang out more with your dog and teach good behavior and manners all day long.

Phobic Behaviors

Fear and phobias differ in that phobic behavior is excessive. Fear responses tend to be acute, and some degree of recovery (resolution) of the fear occurs.

Phobic behaviors have been thought to be less founded because there is no tactile physical experience prior to the response. An example of this is thunder phobic behavior. The dog, although not physically harmed, will exhibit phobic behavior at the sound of thunder.

Fear, on the other hand, is seen as a response to a learned stimulus. An example of this is the dog who was hit by a car, and now shies away from vehicles as they approach.

Shaking

Dogs that are shaking should be examined by a veterinarian to rule out any organic involvement. Once the shaking has been deemed behavioral, one must look at exactly when it occurs, and for how long it lasts. It is important not to bring attention to this shaking so as not to reinforce attention-seeking shaking. After the trigger has been identified, the source of the therapeutic behavioral treatment may begin.

I had a case of a young cocker spaniel that was happy and healthy but over a period of two months began shaking every time his owner prepared to leave the house. Upon taking a history of the events leading to his owner's departure, I learned that his "mom" whined at him, telling him that he would be okay and not to worry because "Mommy will be right back." The pup could have cared less that she was leaving until she made an issue of it. He began to show signs of anxiety when she began her speech by shaking and trembling. The trigger in this case was his owner's pre-departure lecture. Once his mom stopped making such a big deal about leaving, he stopped his shaking and trembling.

Hiding (Refusal to Go Outdoors)

Hiding is seen as a response to fear. Do not try to grab the collar of a dog that is attempting to hide. When a dog is afraid, he may fight to maintain the hideout, where he feels safe. When this hiding becomes chronic, with the dog spending more and more time in this hiding space, then it may be time to intervene. Begin with keeping a leash on your dog. You must be able to easily get him without calling him out of the spot. Take him outside, and keep your talking to a minimum. Bring a favorite toy outside with you or a great food treat and have about fifteen minutes of fun. Come back indoors and leave the leash on the dog. Prevent him from running back into his hiding area and continue trying to feed him from your hand or play with his favorite toy. If he is too worried to play, allow him while still on the leash to go to his hiding spot. You may name his spot as "go to your place" or some similar command so that you may eventually gain control of the hiding spot.

After days of being able to physically move your dog to the outside using the leash with no verbal cue, begin to say "wanna go out?" before using the lead to move your dog to the outside. Remember to reward your dog well for his positive motions toward the doorway and away from his hiding spot. Repeat frequently and you will accomplish your goal of less hiding and more confident behavior.

Noise and Thunder Phobia

Dogs that fear loud noises and thunder tend toward weak nerve thresholds overall. Noise phobic behaviors are, to some degree, counterconditionable behaviors. To what degree you can desensitize or countercondition your dog may depend upon several factors. Understanding your dog's nerve threshold along with finding the volume that triggers the fearful response are two keys to your dog's eventual behavioral therapy.

One form of conditioning requires that you begin by making only low-level sounds that your dog can cope with, such as dropping a small spoon off the kitchen table or wrapping a cap gun in a large towel several times before firing, while giving some sort of positive reinforcement for the tolerance. The volume and duration of the noise will be increased slowly over a period of several weeks. If the motivation is sufficient you can do wonders for this type of problem. Have patience and continue this process at random, even after it appears to have been resolved, for surely a dog with this type of phobia may have reoccurrences.

Thunder phobic behavior can be a devastating experience not only for the dog but also for the owner. I have seen dogs react in what appears to be sheer panic at the sound of rain, which they associate with thunder. Owners watch their poor dog running through the house in a panic or find him trembling under the bed or hiding in a closet and do not know how to comfort him. Attempting to reassure the noise phobic dog with soothing talk only reinforces the dog's fear. Giving tranquilizers after the storm begins usually results in a dog that is "half in the bag" roughly two hours after the drug has been given. These drugs may keep your dog sedated for many hours. The problem is that the storm may have ended before the medication even kicked in. When tranquilizers are used, it has been my experience that they are not very effective in controlling the fear, therefore I prefer to make every effort to avoid using medications in cases of this phobic behavior. Conditioning via desensitization or counterconditioning are the tools of choice. Tapes and CDs are available with thunder and gun sounds. These tapes are played at minuscule volumes during meals daily. The volume is raised up very slowly until the fearful response is no longer triggered. This problem may be even more difficult to resolve, though, because the barometric pressure may play a part in the fearful response. Not exactly something we have control over in order to help us with the conditioning.

Fear of Children

Years ago I had an interesting case with a police officer and her Gordon setter. One morning the friendly dog had burst out of the front door when he saw a nine-year-old girl standing on the curb awaiting the school bus. As the setter ran toward her to greet her, the little girl became frightened at the sight of this large dark dog running to where she stood and began to scream in fear. The dog's owner was running down the lawn, yelling to the girl not to be afraid, that the dog was friendly. The girl's mother heard the screams and came running at the same time toward the two, also yelling. The mother was yelling at the dog and the dog owner was yelling at the girl. By the time the mother and owner reached the girl and dog there was pandemonium. The mother grabbed her daughter, the owner grabbed her dog, and a few less than wonderful words passed between them. The dog went home, the girl went to school, and the mother went back to her house. From that day forward, the dog was intensely aggressive toward children. The dog became frightened of children after this single extremely hectic event. The dog was able to be rehabilitated with a little work, but it must be understood that once a dog is so afraid of children that it clearly will bite, this dog should no longer have access to children unless closely supervised. I do not wish to complicate the issue, but it really was all the tumult that scared the dog in the first place. If you create a situation in which it seems as though there is something wrong with children, then in the dog's mind, there is something wrong with children, and you may have helped in creating the problem. You must tread carefully here. If your dog is not supervised and attacks someone, then you open yourself to liability. If you are overexcited and nervous around your dog and children you may create a problem. This is obviously a tricky area, so be careful.

I know dogs that have had good reason to fear children because they were tormented by kids from the other side of a fence. I have seen dogs that simply possessed very active defense drives, and this made them unsafe around children.

Fear of Dogs

In Puppies You may find your puppy is not social toward other dogs. It may be that either your dog was taken too early from its mother and littermates, or the littermates may have been much larger and stronger than yours, leaving your pup socially apprehensive. I have seen very dominant puppies separate themselves from littermates and, on their own terms only, solicit play. I have seen puppies that manifested their strong defensive drives in this nonsocial behavior pattern.

I have helped some of these puppies by simply not allowing them to run away when approached by other puppies. On rare occasions, the puppy would actually attempt to bite the other pup. Most often, having the puppy confront the fear has been extremely helpful in resolving the defensive social aggression.

In Adult Dogs When grown dogs show fear of other dogs, I am not optimistic that this fear can be resolved. Once seeded, this fear appears to overwhelm affected dogs. Since resolution is not always possible, management may be the way to go.

Keeping your dog on a leash in public will help. While on a leash, it is helpful to teach your dog how to focus on you in the presence of other dogs. Your dog should not be allowed to run free off a lead in the park because at any minute a dog may show up and cause a fear response that may cause your dog to bolt into the road or simply run away. In a controlled situation, perhaps a fenced-in yard, you may be comfortable with your dog having off-lead exercise. A fenced-in school yard with a gate that you can close will do just fine for short runs or fast walks. Always be aware of what is around you at all times to prevent any accidents.

The use of a head halter is often useful in controlling fearful dogs. A dog can feel secure when it is being controlled by the face. His options disappear, and he proudly follows his owner's lead. This is how it should be.

Training a behavior such as "down-stay" provides us with a bit of control around other dogs too. "Down-stay" is incompatible with running away.

Fear of Men

Dogs may be afraid of men because of past unpleasant experiences. If a dog has been traumatized, the issues to be concerned with are: did the event have physical or psychological consequences? Did the dog recover from the trauma, and if so, how long did it take for him to recover from the event? Has the fear of men increased over time?

This fear might also be the result of a total lack of contact with humans during his critical socialization period.

A dog shouldn't usually generalize a fear of one man to a fear of many unless the dog has had multiple traumatic events revolving around men, or the one trauma was significant enough to prevent recovery.

I have used desensitization and counterconditioning in these cases with good success. You will need to find many "dog people" to help you with this therapy in that the more exposure your dog ultimately gets, the better the success rate.

As with all effective processes, you must find the early triggers and begin there. When your dog sights a man, begin soliciting focus toward you. Be sure to greatly reward your dog for that focus. Many repetitions are required to produce a dog that is willing to focus on the handler when a strange man is in sight.

When you begin, the man should be a great distance away in order to achieve focus from your dog. You will be working toward getting closer and closer to the man. Before we pressure your dog with being close to the man we want to first teach a simple behavior like "sit." During this the man should be quiet, nonthreatening, and nonconfrontational. You must require the sit at the early stage of this work. Using the sit position helps to settle your dog as well as create a better platform for your focus training. When your dog is ready and focusing on you, the man may approach quietly and offer your dog a treat. You should free your dog of its focus command and allow it to eat the treat from the man. If your dog is too afraid, then move farther away from the man, and then have him throw the treats from a distance. As your dog comes to expect these treats he will begin to tolerate the man's presence. Your dog will eventually look forward to the approach of men, generalizing that he will receive a reward from them.

Always be careful with a dog that is phobic. Phobic dogs may bite from the breakdown in their nerve thresholds. The humane thing to do in the case of a phobic dog is to try your best to work through the dog's problem and get your veterinarian's advice regarding possible drug intervention during the course of behavior therapy. Many dogs do very well with this treatment. If it works, keep in mind that it is a good idea to keep up the socialization or the dog can break down and resume the old behavior. If after all your efforts, the dog is extremely unreliable despite professional help, then perhaps the dog should be placed in a situation that would not evoke the response. If there was a place where men never visited, then you have a home. Containing a dog like this is possible with the help of safe indoor and outdoor enclosures. Should this kind of control not exist and we are dealing with a large, dangerous, and phobic dog, then we may have to look at euthanasia to prevent civil liability.

Separation Anxiety

Separation anxiety is a very common problem in the dog world. Dogs will frequently manifest their fear of being alone through inappropriate behaviors. Dogs are highly social animals and must learn to tolerate being left alone for extended periods. This problem is not defined by age or breed.

When a dog is afraid of being alone, he may act depressed or increase his activity level while you practice your daily departure ritual. It is important for you to notice what there is about your morning routine that the dog recognizes as a predeparture trigger so that you may use this information to countercondition the already anxious behavior. When a dog cannot settle himself down when you are putting on your shoes, then it will be nearly impossible for him to settle down after you actually leave the house. If your shoes trigger the anxiety, then your job becomes one of putting on *and* taking off your shoes long before you actually depart from home. Practice this seemingly silly task when you have zero intention of going out. Just practice the trigger, giving no attention to your probably anxious dog during the process. Every trigger must be addressed. Car keys, topcoat, keys locking the door, whatever it is, disassociate it from the departures. Practice the ritual, and do not walk out the door until you have worked every early trigger.

Spite is the common term used by the unknowing when their dog becomes destructive or eliminates in the house when left alone. These owners tend to be very angry with their dogs. Owners of dogs that bark and howl when alone find it is easier to resign themselves to the fact that the dog is uncomfortable, not actively spiteful. I have seen situations where a dog has been comfortable when alone, but without any obvious changes to his environment or schedule, the dog has, for lack of a better term, "anxiety attacks." These events were not consistent and therefore a bit more difficult to eliminate because of a lack of understanding of the triggers that prompted the separation event.

Psychotropic medications have been helpful in relieving the chemical reactions associated with separation anxiety. The most common type of drug used is the tricyclic antidepressant. Veterinary intervention into separation cases is often helpful to rule out any organic problems triggering the separation event. It is your veterinarian or veterinary behaviorist who may prescribe the appropriate medications. Behavioral conditioning generally takes weeks or months to resolve this problem, although I have had cases resolve in shorter periods.

Fear of Environment (Objects)

When you take your pup for a walk and he sees a garbage can on its side for the first time, he is apt to be petrified. Many owners bend down and unknowingly reinforce the fear by attempting to soothe the pup with kind words and gentle strokes. Whether it is a place or thing that scares your dog, you must make him face it. The dog will feel much better after you have helped him to get past the obstacle in question.

When I was in high school gym class, my teacher once demonstrated a vault off of the horse. He positioned his knees on the horse and just leaped off, landing on his feet. I had other ideas of how to exercise and this wasn't one of them. My teacher forced me to throw myself off the horse, and guess what? I landed on my feet, not my face. Point being, it's the same for a dog. Help your dog overcome these problems as soon as you are able to detect them. A stairway is often the object of fear, and I have successfully resolved this problem many times with a variety of solutions. After observing him it was apparent to me that one dog was afraid of slipping, so we carpeted the stairs and taught him to overcome his fear, a few steps at a time. Another solution is to place the dog onto the staircase and use a leash to help him by gently urging him, one step at a time, down the stairs. Exuberant praise along with repetition of this procedure will result in a confident stair climber.

Fear of Cars

Often dog owners think that they own a dog that has motion sickness and that will vomit all over the luxurious interior of the family car. Sometimes they are right, and it is solved by the dog having an empty stomach and taking frequent short rides. Carsick dogs usually get over it quickly when you practice the short-ride routine.

Car phobic behavior may stem from a previous accident, a chronically nauseated rider, or perhaps something as simple as a noisy muffler or backfire. Bringing the dog to within sight of the car, giving him a treat, and then bringing him back to where he feels comfortable is a good place to begin this conditioning. Eventually, he may actually be eating his meals in the car. The dog will graduate to eating in the idling car, and soon will be eating in the moving car. The meals are obviously removed from the car once the dog has shown no reluctance to jump in. If your dog has motion sickness, then feeding will not be the way to go. Veterinarians can offer a motion sickness remedy for those so afflicted.

Compulsive Behaviors

Barking

Barking is a normal behavior of dogs. Some breeds are more inclined to bark than others under certain circumstances. Barking at strangers may be normal for a shepherd, whereas barking at squirrels is normal for a Jack Russell terrier.

Barking can become very annoying when it is nonstop. Your neighbors will testify to this, even if you deny it. Barking is also stressful for your dog. This obsession is difficult to resolve when the anxiety level of the dog is high. Treating the apparent cause of the barking is always the first place to begin. Dogs who have separation anxiety frequently bark as a manifestation of their fear of being alone. This barking may become obsessive. Treatment involves basic conditioning previously explained in the section on separation anxiety.

You should try to understand why dogs bark when they are isolated in backyards, garages, or basements. Clearly a dog that is constantly barking would rather be with you than where he is. If your dog is banished to these areas from the rest of the house because he has a problem, fix the problem. If he jumps on furniture, fix the jump. If he steals food from the countertops, fix his thievery. Teach your dog responsible freedom in your home.

There are remote shock units available that are very effective in curtailing chronic barking. The problem is that when the *cause* of the barking is not addressed, your dog will substitute the barking behavior for another behavior. I have seen dogs switch from chronic barking to self-mutilation. I have had cases where dogs have bitten their owners after receiving a correction from a bark device. Remote units are sometimes helpful, but I recommend that you hire a professional to assess the problem and offer you expert eyes so that you can take care of the barking problem from its roots.

Spinning

Spinning in circles can become an obsessive behavior. I have watched dogs spin at different rates of speed and spin in one direction or both directions. Spinning can result from various triggers, but I have seen some spin without any apparent stimulus.

I always send a dog with a history of spinning to the veterinarian for a neurological evaluation. If the dog comes back with a clean bill of health, the problem is said to be a behavioral issue. Spinning can be interrupted by giving the dog a favored chew toy to relax with. Placing the dog in a static position, such as "down-stay," will prevent a dog from spinning.

Most often, spinning is treated as a compulsion using psychotropic medications along with behavioral therapy.

Self-mutilation

Self-mutilation often looks like an allergic skin problem to the dog owner. People observe their dogs lick and bite at various areas of their bodies and often have their dogs treated by the veterinarian for a medical condition. It is generally not until one specific lesion is clearing up and another one is quickly caused that a behavioral diagnosis is pursued.

Self-mutilation may be caused by various physical ailments, and it is imperative to rule out any organic causes for the dog's chewing and mutilating behaviors, prior to considering a behavioral diagnosis and treatment plan.

Some years ago I remember reading about a snow leopard in a zoo that self-mutilated by chronically licking his leg. The leopard licked himself down to the bone, and the zoo veterinarians were puzzled by the behavior and theorized that perhaps there was a chemical component to the behavior. Their curiosity prompted them to use an endorphin blocker, which caused the leopard to stop his licking. This indicated that the animal did in fact get a chemical endorphin release from licking, and since that does feel good, you can understand how this behavior became obsessive.

I am not sure if endorphin is released in all species due to obsessive licking, but it is theorized in dogs. The treatment for dogs would be the same one used with the snow leopard. A morphine antagonist, that is a drug that reverses the effect of morphine, is administered as an endorphin blocker.

Dobermans are a breed with a high incidence of self-mutilation. Flank-sucking behavior is not uncommon in this breed. (The flank is the area behind the rib cage, in front of the hip.) Dr. Nina Shoulberg, a veterinary dermatologist, did a study of lick lesions (a result of obsessive licking) a few years ago and treated her patients with Prozac. I believe the conclusion was that while on the Prozac, the problem resolved itself, but after the dogs were weaned off the medication, many dogs began to obsessively lick again. This is a difficult problem that is best handled using a combination of pharmaceutical agents along with behavioral therapy. Behavioral therapy may be implemented as increased exercise, diet changes, and basic training. It is important to keep your dog close to you so that you can observe his behavior and positively reinforce him when he is not licking. Dogs can learn to lick themselves if the owners give attention to the licking. This case would be attention-seeking behavior with the licking being a means to gain attention. Licking can also be a result of boredom or separation anxiety.

Across the board, treatment generally consists of behavior modification and medication.

Attention-Seeking Behaviors

Limping

For many years I worked with Dr. Martin DeAngelis, a gifted veterinary orthopedist, and had the advantage of assisting with countless exams and procedures. I recall a miniature poodle that required a cruciate (knee) repair on the right rear knee. The surgery went well, and the dog recovered from anesthesia and was sent home the following day. At the one-week recheck the dog was still holding up the right rear leg, but this is not uncommon after only one week. Upon manipulation the knee felt strong, and a recheck appointment was scheduled for two weeks later. At the three-week postop examination the dog was still holding the leg in the air and getting around on three legs. Again upon palpation the knee felt strong. X rays were taken to ensure that the surgical correction had not broken down. The radiograph confirmed that the knee was stable, but still the dog limped around on only three legs. Dr. DeAngelis questioned the owners about allowing her too much activity or letting her run on slippery floors, but the owners were conscientious about such things and had been extremely careful. Further discussion revealed the problematic behavior of her owners. It seems they had been lifting and holding their poodle a lot to "help" her out. They were very accommodating, and when she limped into a room they basically waited on her as if she were a princess. Dr. DeAngelis counseled the owners to stop paying so much attention to this limping and begin to treat her normally. The owners complied but still she held her right leg up in the air. Finally Dr. DeAngelis decided to bandage up her left rear leg to evaluate if she could actually bear weight on it. The dog was able to and showed no sign of pain or apprehension. The good leg remained bandaged for one week, and upon removing the bandage the dog was four-legged again.

Basically, the owners trained this dog to limp and had no idea that she could do so in an attempt to gain attention. It was a fascinating lesson for me.

The moral to the story is: Be careful what you reinforce—you may get it.

Stealing Objects

Commonly, a puppy will pick up a shoe off the floor, which provokes us to chase after him and take the forbidden object away. The dog that is frequently isolated or prohibited from exercise will learn how to vie for negative attention. As I've said, negative attention is better to the dog than no attention at all, hence his stealing articles to solicit your attention.

Pick your issues carefully when training your dog. When your dog has an object that you must retrieve, do not under any circumstances chase him. He can and will outrun you while learning how to achieve attention from you. Ignore the behavior unless the object is dangerous to your dog's health. In this case, replacing the object he is holding in his mouth usually works. When replacement does not work, then you may need to use a can with several pennies in it to startle him into dropping. The "throw can" technique needs to be done so that your dog doesn't see you throw it. The can flew out of the sky and landed near him when he picked up the forbidden object.

Employing the commands "drop it" and "leave it" are helpful with this problem. Teaching the dog to play with only his toys is also important. Having a long line attached to his collar in the house while conditioning your dog out of this behavior eliminates the need for you to chase him to get back whatever he has picked up.

Barking

Barking may stem from your dog's need to receive attention. There is a simple solution—give him attention when he doesn't bark. Do not give attention shortly after he barks because we do not want to reinforce this behavior. Remote collar corrections may help solve this type of barking. Electric shock collars really can be helpful in the right hands when used for the right reasons and when there is a plan for eliminating the original cause of the barking and a plan for discontinuing the use of the remote shock collar. Provide your dog with adequate quality time or else you may have to place him in a home where he can receive quality attention.

Digging

Digging can be great recreation for the lonely dog. Once again, negative attention is better than none. See reasons and treatments for digging in the section in this chapter on Destructive Behaviors.

Jumping

Jumping is most often an attention-seeking behavior. Dogs are reinforced when they are puppies that they will get attention when they jump on you. Because dogs are so social, this may be difficult to correct after months or years of inadvertent positive reinforcement that encouraged the jumping.

My favorite correction for jumping is to teach a great "sit." Dogs cannot be sitting and be on your chest simultaneously. Training the "sit" is covered in the section on canine etiquette in chapter 6.

Feeding/Elimination Behaviors

Anorexia

Anorexia or failure to eat is the first sign of an unhealthy pet in veterinary medicine. Anorexia may be behavioral. When dogs are stressed they will sometimes go "off" feed. I have seen dogs become a bit finicky when it comes to eating, and I have watched owners get on the floor and hand-feed their dogs one kernel at a time. This type of hand-feeding only reinforces not eating from the dish. Once the anorexia is deemed behavioral we must not fall into the trap of cooking special meals for a dog, hand-feeding him, or switching food brands daily.

An interesting case that I had a couple of years ago involved a young female rottweiler owned by a local police officer. The officer was told by a breeder and his veterinarian that his dog would probably gain three to five pounds per week. This bitch was not a great eater, yet her body was always well fleshed with no bony protrusions over her spine or hips. Still her owner was determined to make sure she was going to grow up to meet her full-size potential and fed her whatever she would eat. He had a corner in his home filled with a variety of twenty-pound bags of assorted dry dog foods. His rottweiler would eat one day, then not eat the next. Frustration overcame the owner and he started to force-feed his dog. He was angry when he did this and mumbled assorted things as he shoved the food into her mouth, holding it shut until she swallowed. From that day on, his dog ate less food and would stand over the bowl when he was near her, but was too stressed and wouldn't eat. If he yelled at her, she ran to the bowl but still would only eat a morsel at best, just to comply with her handler. I treated the owner with patience and recommended they go to their veterinarian for a prescription. While the owner was patching up his relationship with his dog, she had been put on a short course of steroids in order to increase her appetite. This worked very well. The dog was weaned off the steroids over a two-week period and afterward she maintained her appetite and ate well, needing no special foods or feeding methods.

Begging

Dogs will beg for affection and attention just as soon or sooner than they will beg for food. Begging for attention may also be considered demanding behavior. Your job here is to be careful about what you reinforce to your dog. If you feed your dog bits of food off your dinner plate, then expect your dog to be sitting at your side and drooling all through every meal. The worst-case scenario is that he is in your lap taking your dinner, and if you try to push him off, he bites you. This is no joke, I've seen it happen.

The feeding ritual should be that your family eats dinner before the dog. Period. If you have the old excuse about how your schedule is erratic and the poor dog needs a routine, then let me remind you that wild dogs may not eat every day, and most dogs are too heavy already. Again, the family eats first.

Begging is a solvable problem whether it is begging for attention or begging for food. Begging is extinguished by *never* reinforcing the behavior. Once a dog has been positively reinforced for nudging your hand, he will nudge away. Do not pet a dog that nudges you.

A dog that is commanded to lie down and stay can't at the same time be in your lap. Train your dog while you are sitting on your couch watching TV or train him while you sit at your dining room table. Practice when there is no food on the table; place your dog in an acceptable area and have him wait there or put him into an absolute "down-stay" position. Release your dog after he has completed his stay so that he knows just how long he is to stay in a down position. He will soon forget about begging.

Stealing Food

Stealing food is a problem that has stumped me once or twice over the years. I resolved the cases not with conditioning tools but with padlocks.

I visited a home to train a young male golden retriever, and while I was there, the client asked me if I wouldn't mind addressing a problem they were having with a four-year-old female golden. I said I'd be glad to. Foolish me. I came armed with an arsenal of remote corrections in my bag of tricks. The situation was that the dog was stealing food from the refrigerator. She would open the door and go to town. I pulled the rubber back where the door meets the frame so that she would get pinched when she scratched and mouthed the door. No problem for her. Next I tried mousetraps inside the refrigerator. Problem was the owner tripped them off and the dog couldn't have cared less. I planted jalapeño peppers with just enough meat to make them look like meatballs, and the teenage son ate them late one night after a concert. He doesn't like me anymore. Still the dog continued on. Then I thought I'd get clever and placed a frying pan on top of the refrigerator and tied the handle to the refrigerator door. When the dog pulled the door open this pan was supposed to fall down and startle her. I went outside and waited for a while, peering through the window, and sure enough, she started to work the door. When it started to open she suddenly looked up. I guess she heard the pan slide on top of the refrigerator. From that moment on, she negotiated how much she could open the door without pulling the pan down. Amazing. In the end a strong padlock was placed on the door. Most cases aren't this extreme, and one of the previously mentioned methods should work.

Other modern options include using remote collars for this type of stealing. Obviously, not giving the dog the opportunity is the first rule. This opportunity should only be given as a setup for correction purposes.

Coprophagy

Coprophagy is the most disgusting habit a dog can have. Sorry, I know the routine that it's the mother's job to clean up after her puppies, but c'mon. I do not want to smell the breath of a dog who makes a habit of eating the stools of others or even its own.

Multiple theories run amok on this topic. Some people say that competition starts it. When the pups are young, breeders run to clean it up quickly so that the puppies do not dance in their own mess. The puppies soon learn to rush for the stool in an effort to "win it." Another theory is that it's a nutritional problem. Others will say the dog is hiding its stools from the owner or eating them outdoors as a sort of territorial safety measure. I've heard so many explanations, but the simple truth is owners don't care where it comes from. They just want it eliminated (so to speak).

I have used commercial products attempting to turn the stools rancid with mixed success. These products are sometimes available through your veterinarian and are mixed with the dog's food. It's worth a try. Good quality nutrition can only help, so be sure your dog's diet is balanced.

Vitamins can't hurt and I have suggested Super Blue Green Algae with regular success. Supervising the walks will at least control the behavior; command your dog to "leave it," and continue on your way.

Pica

Pica is the term used for the ingestion of foreign objects. Dogs with pica may swallow just about anything that'll go down. It is difficult to say what causes it.

I had a case where a young female standard poodle was truly compulsive about grabbing and swallowing just about anything she could find. The dog had eaten sponges out of the sink, kids' toys, pillows, socks, rocks and dirt . . . I could go on. I called my friend Dr. Jane Bicks, a veterinary nutritionist, and she advised me to have the dog's diet changed from two meals daily to free feeding, with a low-protein and high-fiber food. In a matter of days the dog appeared much calmer, and over the weeks, the dog's behavior was normal, with the dog only chewing that which was provided by the owner as a treat.

Dogs may eat foreign objects as a result of organic disease, such as pancreatic insufficiency or malabsorption syndrome. Psychomotor seizures can also create inappropriate ingestion of materials. Organic disease must be ruled out by a veterinary exam prior to implementing diet and/or behavioral changes. All too often the pica dog ends up in the veterinarian's surgery room having foreign bodies removed.

Appendix II, which is on nutrition, discusses dietary options for a few training and behavioral issues.

House Soiling

House soiling in the adult, otherwise housebroken, dog should always be examined medically to insure a healthy dog. Eating and drinking habits should be clearly documented to help arrive at a correct behavioral diagnosis.

House soiling may be the result of a separation problem or it may be a territorial issue. In any case, the treatment is determined by the cause. Territorial dogs are confined or neutered. Dogs feeling separation anxiety are conditioned back to comfort. Psychogenic polydipsic dogs (excessive drinkers) will be treated medically as well as behaviorally.

Submissive/Excitement Urination

If your dog is one of these wetting-at-the-sight-of-visitors types, or sprinkling your work shoes with joy when you arrive home, then listen up. You cannot discipline a dog for this behavior. Your dog exhibits this behavior either because you are much too powerful in your demeanor toward your dog or you overstimulate your dog too much with hectic play sessions or your dog has not been adequately socialized. In any case, punishment is ludicrous. Never clean this urine up in front of the dog, because it only increases the dog's anxiety, creating a vicious cycle of elimination. The urine or stool must be cleaned up before the dog is introduced back into the area where the mishap occurred. Punishment may very well bring out defensive aggression, and a confrontation should be avoided.

Issues that create excitement need to be conditioned to an acceptable level whereby the dog can maintain bladder control. Practice will help you to overcome the problem. Remember: you need patience—no punishment—and a little time.

Territorial Urination

In the adult intact male dog, acts of territorial urination are not uncommon. Leg lifting is directly tied to territorial behavior and has a strong hormonal component.

I have been very successful in aborting this behavior with surgical castration in the male dog. Other methods of extinguishing this behavior include confinement and strict supervision of the offending dog, until such time that the behavior has been eliminated. The dog that lifts his leg in the house cannot be unattended for he will surely mark your furniture or walls if left alone. When you can catch a dog in this act, you may verbally show your displeasure and then take your dog outside for a correct elimination.

Behaviors Treated by Psychotropic Drug Therapy

Sometimes commands, conditioning, and neutering aren't enough in the cases of severe problem behavior, and medicinal intervention is necessary. But though most people almost always feel that they would rather not use drugs, some cases involving misbehaviors clearly have a chemical component, and the use of psychotropic medications has drastically improved the quality of many animals' lives. I commonly call veterinarians, asking them to consider a behavioral medication as I help the owner establish some sort of training program to accommodate resolution of the problem.

I feel that the drugs used alone would be a temporary solution because as dogs are weaned off medication, many return to their previous behavior. Training or behavioral conditioning must accompany the medications.

These drugs can be used to help treat phobic, aggressive, compulsive, and elimination behaviors. Initially these medications should not be administered on a day when you cannot watch your dog for side effects. Simply as a precaution, most veterinarians prefer to take routine blood tests as an organic baseline for any changes that may occur in the future.

The medications previously used were usually tranquilizers. Most veterinarians were not schooled in the uses of psychotropic medications, and the thought of using Prozac on dogs a few years back would have been considered comical. Who would use psychotropic drugs on pets? Now, it's commonplace.

I had a case about two years ago where a dog that suffered with separation anxiety barked and howled throughout the entire day. Barney's "mom" worked all day and returned home to find notes taped to her door from her neighbors complaining about Barney's barking. In her haste to eliminate this barking, she bought an antibarking collar that would offer Barney a shock treatment each time he barked, hoping that he would learn to be quiet. Barney's owner came home after his first day of wearing the antibarking device to find a large electrical burn on Barney's neck as well as an extremely nervous Barney. Initially this dog was afraid of being left all alone, so he barked. After receiving the shock from barking, he became more frustrated and barked more because of the painful device, creating the electrical burns to his skin. Barney was taken to the veterinarian for treatment of his burns and the doctor recommended that the collar not be used again until they consulted with me.

The case became more interesting the very next day, when Barney's owner tried to leave the house; Barney, her normally friendly dog, bit her and stood between his owner and the door, preventing her from leaving the house. Barney's fear of being alone had risen to fear of being hurt while alone. In the dog's mind, if his owner was home, he was safe. When she left home, he was in pain. He did the logical thing—prevent her from leaving. I immediately put the dog on a course of behavioral therapy that included predeparture desensitization and asked the client's veterinarian to prescribe an antidepressant. The electric collar was no longer used and in a matter of a few weeks the dog's fear diminished, resulting in a quiet and, once again, friendly dog.

Medication has become useful in the treatment of phobias, obsessive-compulsive problems, and aggression disorders.

Veterinary science has come a long way in the understanding and application of behavioral medications. Many have come to rely on these medications for very good reason—they work. These medications have been helping people cope for a long time. Now it's time to try and help animals too.

In my practice, the use of medications has aided in making conditioning easier. In some cases, there may not have been the same success without them. Pharmaceutical interaction can be an enormous tool but I take issue with medicating a dog that is not being worked on with behavioral training simultaneously to resolve a problem.

Side effects are something to be aware of when using these medications. Your veterinarian will explain the problems with certain medications and advise you as to the best way to avoid any subsequent problems. Choice of medications is usually determined by your veterinarian or behaviorist.

6.

Interactive Training for Puppies and Dogs

Beginnings

The creation of anything destined for greatness relies on its sound foundation. As kids, great musicians were tortured by their parents into practicing. The most primary scales were gone over endlessly, slowly, and meticulously. An analogy to this would be *Run Spot Run* for early readers. The same holds true for just about any artist and their work. Think of yourself as an artist and that your project is to build the perfect dog. You will use your imagination as well as a little science. This will be a labor of love, so prepare your tools and yourself. By the end, your finished masterpiece will be your best friend.

Effective teaching may begin after a few ground rules are put in place. The first rule has to do with handling. Your dog must accept being handled. Dogs that struggle or attempt to bite while being handled must be taught to accept physical contact. This is easy with puppies and a bit more difficult with some adult dogs. Specifically, you must be able to touch your dog everywhere. You must be able to check his ears or hold his feet.

Handling your dog's feet, ears, and routine grooming help us to recognize early signs of tactile sensitivity or aggression. Building a compliant dog who obeys commands with "no questions asked" comes from his respect for you. Any resistance from your dog in handling his body must first be resolved through systematic handling procedures.

Being able to put your hands on your own dog without fear of being bitten is essential. Fractious dogs need to be conditioned into allowing their owners to handle them under essentially any conditions. The techniques used to establish control and handling require that the dog be on a leash and oftentimes the use of a head halter or muzzle so that the dog's mouth is controlled so as to maximize your control. Treats are offered to the dog as it allows handling of its feet, ears, etc. Practice sessions are performed daily until there is a trust between the owner and the dog. Once established, training becomes easier.

The idea of having a well-trained dog is very appealing. A dog that walks along at your side, never pulling on the leash, or better yet, walks nicely with no leash at all, seems to be the dream of choice with my clientele.

Let's examine the procedures for getting this well-trained dog out of your dreams and into your house.

Timing

It is said that timing is everything. Although it may not be everything in dog training, it is very important. Most dog trainers have dealt with nervous or aggressive dogs whose owners have "consoled" the dog exhibiting the behavior and thereby inadvertently reinforced the very behavior they wish to extinguish.

If you do not want Rover barking at the door, then stop saying "it's okay" when guests arrive or when your dog is lunacy on two legs, unless you want your dog to get hysterical and jump all over everyone who enters your home. Stop with the "it's okay" when it is clearly not okay. I know what you are thinking. You feel that telling your dog "okay" will calm him down, and you want to assure him that life is peachy. In reality, however, if you say "It's okay, it's Uncle Louie" to your dog, who is aggressively barking at the door, when Uncle Louie comes over, your dog will assume that you like his aggressive barking and maybe it is okay to bite Uncle Louie.

In terms of timing and rewards, I praise and/or feed the millisecond I see the dog thinking about doing the right thing. This is how I begin shaping behaviors. Once your dog is interested in the way you plan to reward it, you can wait the dog out, a little at a time, until the dog shows the desired behavior. If a "sit" is crooked, you may either fix it with a hands-on approach and reward, or just reward any sit. Hold back reinforcement after the second or third repetition unless your dog gets closer to a straight sit. Eventually your dog will sit straight, knowing that it is the only way to get the reward.

The absence of the reward is a cue to your dog that his behavior is not yet correct. One benefit of this technique is that the dog is "working you over" for the reward, you do not have to physically handle the dog in order to teach the position.

Rewards

Rewards have to make sense to your dog, not you. If you cheat, your dog will not consistently respond because of the harsh compulsion necessary to obtain his compliance. Conversely, compliance can be obtained with timely use of strong drive fulfillment, be it hunger or prey.

Food Food rewards work well for teaching exercises, especially when you are dealing with a hungry dog that has tremendous food drive. When using food rewards, be sure to make certain to use special food and try to vary the type and amount during reinforcement. Also remember that once the behavior has been learned, intermittent reinforcement is more powerful than consistent reinforcement. Space out the number of treats given as rewards. It is fine for your dog to expect a treat, it is just that sometimes it will not be there. Most dogs are willing to respond in the very hopes of the food reward. The dog that responds only to food and is otherwise hearing impaired has a basic relationship problem to be dealt with before further training can effectively begin.

Praise Praise is an interesting area of the reward system. Dogs surely relish praise, but are they willing to work for it? Years ago when the six-foot leash and slip training collar were the key tools of the trade, verbal praise was a large part of what it took to recover the dog's happy attitude after the leash and collar corrections. When compulsion was used to enforce a command, then generous praise was freely administered at the very second of compliance. This works when the praise is genuine and exuberant. Praise works when the handler can see the correct behavior coming down the pike and begins to verbally encourage the dog to continue the desired behavior. Praise is very bad when the owners cannot see that all the dog is showing is bad intent and the dog is receiving the praise for all the wrong reasons. Let's face it, no one can read minds, but you can learn to anticipate a few behaviors when you are able to read your dog well.

There is a bit of controversy over whether dogs prefer physical or verbal praise. I personally feel that both are appropriate. The key here is when and how much to offer at any given time. My dear friend Carol Lea Benjamin says that you have provided excellent touch when your hand gets warm from the body heat of your dog. Sounds right to me. Although I have encountered dogs who prefer verbal praise, I think it was because they were a bit nervous. These are threshold issues!

Note that eye contact is often sacrificed when physical contact is made. I have noticed many dogs lose eye contact with their owners at the very second their hands touch them. Dogs train much better with soothing words rather than touch, because they can maintain their focus.

When offering verbal praise, the pitch of your voice is very important. Men in general offer deep sounds for praise that may resemble growling. Therefore, a deep voice may not be looked upon as positive to your dog, whereas high-pitched sounds indicate to your dog that a job was well done. When in doubt err on the side of praise for a job well tried if nothing else.

Tug-of-War Although tug-of-war games are generally shunned in my business, I strongly feel the opposite. Many dogs love tug-of-war more than life itself. They would be willing to perform any number of behaviors for a simple game of tug. I think it is silly not to use the drive. I also teach a dog when to "take it" and when to "drop" and/or to "leave it." Since I have total control of this game early on, why would my dog suddenly become possessive or aggressive over the tug toy? The way I see it, multiple commands and gentle handling are more apt to create aggression than tug-of-war. Playing tug-of-war gives you the opportunity to greatly reward your dog with a game that keeps him close to you, instead of throwing a ball, which has him running away from you. Tug-of-war shows your dog your strength, which is not a bad thing for your dog to be aware of. Others may feel it is better to create conflict with hostile confrontation rather than show power while playing. Use a dog's high drive for obedience to achieve your own ends.

Training Equipment

For Puppies

Harnesses, collars, leashes, crates, toys, and treats are all in the mix of what you need to maximize on your dog's formal education. Building a sound training foundation is difficult when there are no tools available, so it is best to be prepared for the job before induction. Many people enjoy collecting "tools"; I saw a collar being sold at the Westminster Kennel Club dog show benching area for $1,800 that looked like an English mastiff collar from the early 1900s. You need not get too carried away with the tools, but collecting can be fun and fashionable.

Equipment for training puppies may be different from the equipment required to train an adult dog. The tools needed for a dog that has its rudimentary obedience under control is different from those needed for a dog with zero obedience skills. It can be confusing walking into a pet supply store to buy a leash because consumers can be overwhelmed by the liberal selection available. Often a new dog owner's prerequisite for buying a leash and collar has to do with color instead of function. Dogs often learn to be equipment sensitive and easily figure out that when the leash comes out, it's time for a walk. Police dogs used for tracking often begin working their nose the moment the tracking harness goes on. This sensitivity can be wonderful.

Collars and Leashes While your puppy is as young as seven to ten weeks of age, I recommend that soft cotton collars be put on and off the puppy's neck several times during the day to help the pup adjust to the sensation of wearing the collar. Once your puppy is no longer stopping every two feet and scratching at his neck, you can move along and attach a light soft line to his collar and let him drag the line around the house. You must supervise this event so he will not get tangled up or eat the line. Generally, after a couple of days the puppy will run around the house and not be intimidated by the dragline. This is the time for you to pick up the line occasionally and walk your puppy around the house. If your pup stops walking, do not pull him, instead induce him with friendly gestures such as a waving hand or "Mickey Mouse" talk until he gets up and walks. At this time you will praise him wildly for moving along with you. In order to continue making his leash time positive, it is a good idea to drop the line at times so that your puppy will have no opposition from tension on the line. When you notice him moving well along with you, break into a play session. The more comfortable your pup is with the leash the better it will be for both of you in the very near future. If you practice this exercise in your home with your young puppy, then it will pay off when you go for your outdoor walks.

I prefer that puppies wear long light lines for two reasons. First, a long line conditions your puppy to believe that you have influence at a great distance. Second, short leashes will almost always create forging at the end of the line from the opposition of the tight line. Cotton, nylon, leather, and coated steel cable are all possibilities for a comfortable long line. The forever favorite six-foot training leash will be discussed later in the training exercise section of this chapter. I like the extendible-type leashes for bathroom walks and training the "come" command, although they do not provide very good control in busy situations.

Crates I have become a firm believer in crate training over the years. The great advantages of crate training a puppy are that it provides a safe place for the puppy away from the routine daily tumult, prevents you from attempting to overtrain your puppy, and teaches your puppy to hold its stools and urine until you provide him with the appropriate elimination spot. Crates come in a variety of styles. Wire collapsible

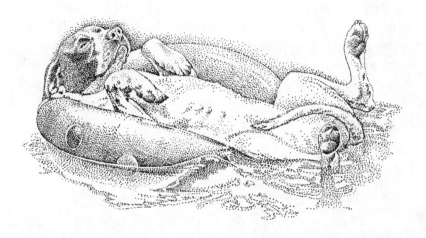

crates are popular as well as the plastic airline-type carriers. There are advantages to both: the wire crate offers better ventilation and visual freedom. The wire crates also usually break down and are easy to store when not in use. Many wire crate manufacturers produce a commercial divider to allow you to make the living space larger as your dog grows in size and responsibility. Plastic crates are usually airline approved and are necessary for dogs traveling by plane. Puppies of the large-breed variety may need several of these crates during their growth and development. They are difficult to section off and make smaller, but they tend to be a bit less expensive than some wire types. I have found the plastic airline crates more difficult to escape from and easier to clean.

Crates should be placed in an area of your home that is frequented by your family. Dogs do not fare well when isolated, thus the kitchen seems to be a popular spot. Kitchen floors are usually easy to clean, so this is a good reason for containing a new dog here. So the kitchen is a good spot, if you have space for the crate.

Toys Puppies love toys, so if you provide them they will play with them forever. I have seen dogs who were deprived of toys as puppies, and they tend to look at these playthings like they were the man on the moon. Toys play a big part in training dogs. When your dog's drive for play has been reinforced then your formal training will look crisp, versus the dog whose obedience is correct yet appears flat from lack of play reinforcement.

Puppies should get used to feeling a wide variety of sensations in their mouths. (Hands are not included.) Hard rubber toys in various shapes are always safe and can be fun. Balls that are large enough not to be swallowed are good entertainment. Rope toys are enjoyable because puppies like to tug. Tug games are not for children to play with the family dog, but if adults have good control of the game it can be terrific fun.

There are toys on the market that are hollow and can be stuffed with treats, acting as an intermittent reinforcer as your dog plays and chews it. Teething discomfort can be remedied using frozen bagels, ice cubes, or frozen pressed rawhide bones.

Remote-Training Devices

Monitors. When first training your dog to be responsible in your home, you want to be aware the moment an inappropriate behavior occurs because corrections long after the fact are worthless. As a behavior is occurring is the time you can teach your dog right from wrong. There are commercially manufactured motion sensitive devices that blurt out a sound to let you know that Rover is in the wrong place and I have even seen elaborate camera systems designed to "spy" on mischievous pets. If your dog is sneaking up onto counters, tables, and furniture, these sensor devices might be worthwhile.

Audible. There are a wide variety of audible remote devices on the market. Some have ultrasonic frequencies that are inaudible to humans, while others are detectable by the human ear. There are audible hand-held units that are pressed by you for off-leash control, and others that emit the sound when motion sensors are remotely triggered by your dog.

The distance that each unit will be effective should be taken into account. Ultrasonic units are most effective at the shortest distance and lose efficacy as distance increases. I have seen a few dogs show little to no reaction to these units at any distance, yet other dogs are extremely sensitive as far as twenty-five feet away. Keep in mind that the units that squelch audible sounds will scare you too when you press the button. I used to use boat horns to get focus from dogs that were running away from me. The problem was that I ended up getting focus from *everyone* within a one-mile radius.

Physical. Physical correction tools are amazingly effective. They include electrically charged mats, mousetrap-type devices, and horrifically odoriferous products such as ammonia or pepper. Setups include a wide variety of inventive procedures as well. For example, place a small bit of bread on your countertop and run a few strips of double-sided carpet tape along the edge. When your dog jumps up onto the counter and gets his feet stuck he will not be quick to return to the countertop. Some dog breeds are less tactile and sensitive and may require a stronger correction. Electric mats offer a few levels of stimulation, and when your dog puts his feet on it, it will sting. Remember, to the dog you should not appear involved in this. The sting came as a result of your dog's behavior, which is unrelated to you. Say nothing or if anything console the dog when it comes to you for safety. You remain safe to your dog as the counter begins to appear dangerous.

Taste deterrents. It is far better for your dog to learn not to chew because things just don't taste that great, as opposed to you screaming "I'll kill you if you chew."

Sheep ranchers were having coyote problems in the Midwest. The ranchers wanted to shoot the coyotes, but the animal rights people would not permit this to occur. An alternative method was approved. The majority of sheep were removed from the pastures and the remaining sheep were injected with a chemical that made the coyotes extremely nauseated. In a matter of days, they were seen chasing rabbits, running right past the sheep. If sheep ranchers can do it, you can do it.

Please do not poison your dog, but understand the concept. If the dog finds your dinner plate unsatisfying when you leave the table to get something in the kitchen, after a while he will stop looking at your dinner as a possibility. A trip down the ethnic food aisle of your favorite grocery store will net you a few items that your dog will not appreciate. Jalapeño peppers might work, wasabi could do it, or perhaps it's horseradish for your dog. Distasteful but nontoxic is the key to success.

Commercial products to deter chewing are available in spray and cream form. They usually work well. Conversely, I have found that the sprays that claim to repel dogs from certain areas do not work very well.

For Adult Dogs

With age, maturity, and growth, equipment use is changed from the soft and frequently colorful puppy equipment to more functional attire.

Leashes The length and width of a leash has to do with the height of the handler and the size and weight of your dog. A tall handler with a small breed of dog will need a very long leash in order to keep the leash slack enough to offer comfort and taut enough to have control of his dog. A short handler will need a short lead if they have a large-breed dog. For example, a person who is five feet ten inches tall with a dog sixteen inches high, weighing thirty pounds, would pick a six-foot leash that is one-half inch wide. Heavier dogs need wider, stronger leads.

I prefer harness leather leashes over latigo (typical) leather although latigo is strong enough for most breeds of dog. I also would rather my obedience leash be braided on both ends with a quality brass snap and no stitches or rivets.

When I use a lead for protection training, I prefer the lead to be double stitched and riveted. These leads are one-half inch thick and three-quarters of an inch wide and four to six feet in length.

Cotton. I have always used these leads for their durability and cost-effectiveness. They are a comfort in your hand and are easy to find in any local pet supply store. You should still look for the leash with the brass clip. It may cost a bit more but is apt to last longer.

Nylon. Nylon leashes are very strong but can be a little rough on the hand if your dog forges on its leash. Advantages for a puppy are that nylon is hard to chew up, therefore there will be less mouthing on the lead. If necessary, the leash is porous enough to soak in taste deterrent and is washable.

Chain. Chain leashes definitely curb mouthy leash behavior. These leashes come in a variety of sizes. Should you choose a chain lead, be sure to pick one strong enough for your dog. Be sensible and avoid getting a tow truck line for your Yorkie. For most situations I think this is an uncomfortable choice of leads, but some people value their strength. I can't argue; chain leashes do tend to be strong.

Cable. I have seen steel cable lines coated with plastic that have a leather handle and are sold as a leash. I guess it would be difficult for a dog to chew through steel cable, but it looks a bit uncomfortable in the owner's hands. Leashes are most comfortable when the excess can be folded neatly into your hand. This is difficult to do with coated steel cable.

Steel cable works very well as a tie-out cable. This cable also comes in varying degrees of thickness. When leaving your dog out on a cable line, you should be able to supervise your dog or at least keep him in visual contact just in case he becomes tangled or threatened.

Retractable. While the variable length is a great option to have, this leash may fail to give support in a problem situation. The handle can be awkward to manage at times. I have seen owners in New York City allow their dogs to traverse the entire sidewalk on retractable leads, which can be both dangerous and annoying.

The retractable is great for teaching the "come" command because it allows the dog to wander a specific number of feet from you, giving you opportunity to give a command and be able to reinforce it.

Lunge lines. Lunge lines are usually employed by equestrians to exercise their horses. These lines are about twenty-five to thirty feet long and one inch wide and made of cotton, while some are made with leather and steel swivel spring snaps. These are great for use as an outdoor dragline, country walking, or a tracking line. They are fairly inexpensive and are invaluable in terms of controlling at a distance.

Lead lines. Horse lead lines are about eight to ten feet long and five-eighths of an inch around and very strong. These work well as house draglines due to their durability and inexpensive cost. You may have to visit a tack shop to find these.

Body Wear

Collars Collars are often chosen as a fashion statement but these choices should change with your requirements for your dog's training. When you train obedience you should choose one collar; if you are training your dog in protection, you might need another type. This all evolves as your dog becomes more off-lead responsible.

Leather. Leather collars are soft and come in a flat or round shape. They tend to be gentle on your dog's neck, and in general the wider the collar (one and a half to two inches), the more comfortable the fit. The round leather collar is more likely to produce hacking behaviors if your dog forges.

Some collars are sold for training German shepherd dogs, rottweilers, and other competition protection breeds. They are two inches wide and made for comfort during agitation and bite training.

Chain. Chain collars are usually of the slip-choker or pinch-collar variety. These collars are used strictly for training, so once trained, dogs should be outfitted with more comfortable equipment.

The chain slip collar can be a very effective tool when used correctly. If you have one of these on your dog, and he is choking at the end of the leash, take it off. Knowledge of correct usage is essential or the collar is merely abusive. The device is meant to be worn loose on your dog and used adjunctively to voice and body postures. Learning how to use it takes practice and usually professional assistance.

The pinch or prong collar looks barbaric but is a very useful tool when used correctly, and it offers much less potential for injury than the slip collar. The pinch collar is fitted to the neck size for effectiveness. This collar should be used with the aid of a professional in that the discomfort offered by this collar can result in an aggressive overreaction by a dog. But it is a great tool for the right handler and the right dog.

Nylon. As with the nylon leashes, these collars are also very strong. They are great house collars. You can hang your dog's vaccination and identification tags off of them. They are durable, affordable, and available in many colors.

Body harnesses. Body harnesses suggest to the dog that he should pull, because opposition reflexes result in strong forging behaviors. Sled dogs, Seeing Eye dogs, carting dogs, and tracking dogs all wear harnesses. Dogs with these jobs of pulling ahead of their handlers should wear harnesses. If you enjoy being pulled, then be my guest and allow your dog to wear a harness. If you want your dog near you on a walk, then do not use a harness.

New body harnesses have been produced to close on the body of the dog behind the forelegs producing some discomfort when the dog pulls on the lead. They appear somewhat effective, but I am skeptical of their long-term safety and efficacy. I also feel that this harness sends a mixed signal to the dog simply in its design. Pulling promotes pulling. Punishment to the dog via body tension is inappropriate after stimulating the dog to pull. Dogs surely can learn how to appropriately suppress the discomfort by not pulling on the lead, yet I am certain that there are easier ways to teach a dog not to forge on the leash.

Car containment. Body harnesses as car containment devices are excellent and can be purchased commercially. I feel that for a dog's safety in a moving motor vehicle, some type of containment is best. Alternatives are crates, dividers, or affixed leads to a flat collar. If your dog rides free in the car, be careful.

Do not allow your dog to hang halfway out of the windows. It is bad for his eyes. Please do not allow your dog to sit in your lap while you drive, no matter how small the dog. It can be dangerous for both of you.

Head halters. Head halters originated in England and have found a new home in the Unite States. These gentle and very effective bridles are super for large dogs who have small handlers. We know that the dog's head is the weakest part of its body. Why not use this information wisely, and use a device that humanely offers you excellent control, given that most large animals are controlled by their heads. Imagine trying to walk a horse on a leash by the neck; you'd be dragged till you perish. I have successfully trained countless numbers of dogs using this tool. It is wonderful.

Shock. Remote shock collars have been around for a long time. Even years ago the device was commonly used as a means of delivering punishment from a distance. These collars may still be used in an inappropriate manner if the user is unskilled in training and reinforcement techniques. I feel as though the companies who manufacture these collars have in fact come a long way, not only in refining the collars themselves but also in responsibly providing books and videos on correct usage and procedure.

The technique for general training is less compulsive than leash and collar training. Many people are under the impression that only an emotionally strong dog can deal with the stress of a remote collar; this is not true.

I had a case where a young male German shepherd dog named Max had a terrible time maintaining his generally carefree demeanor if his owner administered even the slightest physical pressure on him during training. He would act very nervous and opposed any positional (sit, down, etc.) placement. I worked with his owners using food as his motivator. He worked okay, though not spectacularly, whether he was hungry or not. I tried really hard to tempt him with an array of tasty, aromatic special treats. I also attempted using his favorite toys with only marginal success. If his owner gently placed him in a position, he turned his head away from her and did not want to make eye or physical contact with her. This avoidance lasted sometimes hours at a time. By the time he was nine months of age, he began to really blow off commands when the timing did not suit him. The mistress, who works in the veterinary field and has a nice touch with dogs, began to feel that this dog was losing the very control that would keep him safe, and that a definite recall (which means that he would come when called) was essential to their relationship and Max's safety.

I had his owners order a remote collar and had two training sessions with them. The dog learned on the lowest power setting that his "safe zone" was near the handler. Max learned that it was slightly uncomfortable when he did not turn and run toward his owner after she called him. He ran to her for comfort and safety, not away from her, because it appeared that she could "save" him. They now have a fine dog who obeys off lead 99 percent of the time with great spunk and vigor.

I can only say that I feel that a private session or several private sessions with a professional trainer are in order to best learn how and when to use remote collars.

Bark trainers. Electric antibark trainers are on the retail market as well as the aforementioned handheld remotes.

Antibark collars work well, providing that the dog understands how to shut down the stimulation. As with all remote collars, primary training is essential prior to using an antibark device.

Another issue is learning when and why the dog is barking. Dogs that are barking from stress or anxiety may stop barking while wearing a remote antibark device but will almost certainly displace their stress and form other undesirable behaviors.

I would rather that owners of barking dogs look into the causes of the barking before using an antibarking tool. Addressing the cause can often supply a less drastic and long-term solution.

Invisible boundary fences. These fences have become popular in the suburbs where zoning regulations often prohibit conventional fencing. This form of containment is surely better than no fence at all, but will not keep stray animals out of your yard. Most dogs are readily trained to "respect" the boundary, although some dogs will tolerate the correction to explore the world. Once a dog breaks through to the outside, he would have to take a correction for attempting to return through the boundary line. Funny how most dogs are prepared to take the stimulation in order to escape but not willing to take the same stimulation to return home.

I prefer standard fencing to electric, but again, electric is better than none. In any case, dogs should not be left outside alone for too many hours at a time. It frustrates them, and they will begin barking endlessly or running the perimeter of your property terrorizing passersby.

Muzzles. Muzzles are designed to prevent dogs from using their mouths.

Muzzles come in a variety of types. They can be made of leather, nylon, or coated plastic or steel. Some muzzles are made to keep dogs' mouths fully closed while others allow the dog to pant, bark, and drink water through smaller holes or a wire basket-style face containment. Veterinarians and dog groomers often use the style of muzzle that keeps a dog's mouth closed.

Dog owners that need to control aggression in the home usually choose the basket style that allows their dog to drink and bark. The basket style is used when the muzzle will be on a dog for a number of hours, allowing the dog to pant as a means of sweating.

Muzzles are a great tool to help reduce a tough dog's overall attitude, not to mention to prevent destructive behavior when used in conjunction with training.

Housebreaking

It is essential to most of us that our dogs keep certain areas clean. Dogs that live in rural settings often have fewer constraints than our typical city or suburban house dogs. Our dogs may not relieve themselves in our homes. Some dogs, usually of the toy variety, are trained to use a papered area in the house. This is not being housebroken but rather being paper-trained. Housebroken, by my definition, is not eliminating when you feel the urge to eliminate. Waiting for the opportunity to eliminate in the right spot defines a dog that is housebroken.

Housebreaking begins with crate training. Your dog needs to learn to keep one space clean at a time. Once your puppy shows consistently clean behavior in his crate, and he is no longer teething, it is time to stretch his domain. A baby gate across the kitchen might be the logical next step.

Teaching your dog to be responsible in your entire home is best accomplished by intense and frequent exposure to the environment. The two most common spots dogs choose to mess up in are (1) formal dining rooms (with Oriental carpets), and (2) formal living rooms. These are rooms that nobody ever goes into, except maybe on the holidays or when company comes. Intense exposure means train your dog in the room, feed your dog in the room, and spend time playing with your dog in the room. In order for the dog to respect its cleanliness, the room must appear to be a living space. One room at a time, supervised at first with the dragline in place, just in case you need to influence your friend quickly. Should your dog begin to eliminate in front of you, make a few disgruntled sounds as you quickly run to the correct spot. Praise like crazy when he eliminates in the right spot and then take him back into the space where he messed up with no hard feelings. As a rule it is best to clean up any messes in the absence of your dog. There is no need for your dog to become anxious about what has already happened nor should your dog see you take it as some sort of gift.

When your dog is responsible in your home while you are present, then it is time to progress to short periods of freedom while you are out. Extend the time periods slowly and you will be successful. You can have a housebroken dog. I love the stories of rottweiler owners being burglarized while their fine protection dog was locked in a crate. I am of the strong opinion that dogs should be given as much freedom as they can responsibly handle.

Accidents will happen and when they do there are commercial products that eliminate the stains and odors. These enzymatic products help keep your dog from being able to smell the mishap, and that is the important thing. White vinegar and water works well. Never use an ammonia product because ammonia is a by-product of urine and this odor will attract the dog back to the location.

Crate Training

Teaching to Enter Crate
on Command

It is far better for your puppy to run into his crate on command rather than having to chase, catch, and lock the little guy down. The procedure is as follows:

1. Name the crate. Some possibilities are kennel up, go to bed, box, palace, or condo. You can choose whatever name you wish. Just be sure to name the space to make it easy for your puppy to understand what we are talking about.

2. Sit on the floor in front of the crate with your puppy on a leash. Give your puppy the command "kennel up" and gently push him into the crate. Reward him with a special treat while he is in the crate. Invite him out with a release command such as "free" or "okay" and reward him for coming out as well. Turn him around and repeat the procedure about eight to ten times. The goal here is for your puppy to run into his crate and spin around anticipating the arrival of his treat. Since we have not closed the door yet, there should be no resistance to entering the crate on command. Use this exercise to keep your dog happy in his crate.

3. Do not call your dog by name followed by the "come" command and routinely put him in his crate. He may soon decide not to come to you if he makes a come/crate association. He will avoid you even if there is food involved, so don't do it. Simply get your dog's dragline and lead him to the crate when he is going to be put away for some rest.

4. Next comes the part where we may hear a little vocalization. After you send your puppy into his crate as a training exercise, close the door and sit in a chair near the crate. Wait a couple of minutes and then open the door with a release word. Both of you should leave the area together. Increase the period of time your puppy is expected to stay in his crate, and at the same time, begin to walk around while he is still in his crate, showing him that although he is confined, he is not isolated.

5. If your puppy vocalizes too much, you can cover the crate with an old lightweight sheet, which removes visual stimulation. This usually stops the barking. Be certain to use an old sheet to cover the crate because your dog will surely pull it inside the crate and chew it. If your puppy barks in the covered crate, you can sneak up to the crate and slam the top of the crate with a skillet. It is important that you say nothing and that your dog does not see you do this. If every time he barks this horrendous sound occurs, he will blame his bark for the sound, not you. Barking generally stops almost instantly. Do not allow a barking puppy out of the crate unless you enjoy the sound of hysterical barking.

Sample Crate Schedule

1. First thing in the morning, walk your pup.

2. Bring your puppy indoors and give him some supervised free time, preferably in the kitchen(fifteen to forty-five minutes).

3. Give your dog food and water (free water for fifteen minutes).

4. Walk your dog fifteen to forty-five minutes after eating(young pups within five minutes).

5. After the pup has appropriately eliminated, allow for another supervised free period.

6. Crate for three to four hours.

7. Repeat throughout the day.

This sample does not address socialization, exercise, and training periods, all of which are needed for a well-mannered, healthy dog. Water is only increased to free access as your dog proves his ability to hold his urine.

Paper-training

Puppies and small dogs are often paper-trained. Puppies raised in the city will often be paper-trained until its vaccine status allows for exposure to the outdoors. I have found that several of the toy breeds are best paper-trained as well as trained to eliminate outdoors. They often have problems with their ability to hold, so it is very helpful to have a spot indoors that is okay to use in a pinch. My preference whenever applicable is that your dog go from the crate to the outdoors right from the beginning. I have recognized these variables. Some dogs can't hold for very long and some owners do not walk their dogs often enough.

I have had Maltese and Yorkshire terrier owners build a three-by-three-foot square box with sides one inch high to enclose the paper and well delineate the space. One client turned a knock hockey board upside down and used white paper to prevent her white dog from getting old newspaper print on his coat. I used a rubber tub made for cement mixing lined with shredded paper for an Italian Greyhound I worked with. This training has always worked well for me. Those dogs trained box style have freedom of their homes and are responsible.

Technique for Paper-training

Gate a small room, preferably a bathroom. Dogs naturally will leave their eating and sleeping areas to eliminate. Place a bed, food, and water bowls on one side of the room and the box on the other. There may be a few accidents at first, but eventually your dog will figure it out. Again, do not close the door to this small room because that makes the confinement more isolating and stressful. Once the habit of the box has been established, we can begin to allow the pup out under supervision. We may want to remind him every once in a while, by giving the command "hurry up" and walk him to his box on a leash. Wait until he produces and praise him for doing it. He will learn responsibility a little bit at a time.

Promoting Canine Etiquette

Manners

A well-mannered dog is the greatest pleasure. If you have ever had one, then you know this to be true. I can guess that you know someone with an unruly dog. I will further guess that they love him despite his unruliness. Just imagine the bond that can be created between "dogs and their people" when the dog is perfectly well mannered.

Dogs do not have to be endlessly trained in competition obedience in order to be well-behaved pets. A few simple exercises will help your dog become a cherished member of your family.

Loose-Leash Walking

Loose-leash walking, which is walking on a slack leash, is one of the most pleasurable experiences one can have with a dog. Those who go out for their daily drags would give their molars for a walk in which their arms are not pulled . . . I have had clients diagnosed with bursitis due to chronic inflammation of their shoulder joints attributed to the daily walks taken with Rover.

There are only a couple of things that get dogs to walk pleasantly alongside of you. Either they want to, or you want them to. If your dog wants to, well that's great, it is suggestive of your excellent relationship. If you want him to and he shows reluctance, then you must teach him.

Loose-leash walking is best accomplished using a long line (fifteen feet) and some good treats. Begin by walking relatively quickly to a predetermined location. As your dog passes ahead of you, make a turn right and walk toward another previously spied location. Your dog will pass you again and you will then turn right again, quietly walking briskly along. Talking is not part of this exercise. This exercise is done quietly, no command, no praise, just purposefully walking until your dog runs past you, giving you the opportunity to sneak a right turn on your unfocused dog. When the long line becomes tight, your dog will be looking for where you are. But still do not stop walking. Keep up your speed and don't worry about where the dog or line is. A dog's legs are always getting tangled up, so try not to get so involved with the line placement and keep on going. The point to all of this is that it teaches your dog to follow you. If he misses a turn, it was not your fault, it was his fault, and if you are passive and quiet yet strong in your motion, your dog is going to follow you. Turn, Turn, Turn. The exercise is called posting by some, quartering by others. It works, just practice. Soon you will not be able to sneak away in any direction because your dog will be watching you intently for when the turn is coming. Offer praise and treats just for being close to you.

Training a Good "Sit"

It is interesting to me how 99 percent of the dogs I've met in my life could sit on command. I have watched three-year-olds teach a dog to sit, to my own amazement. The lingering problem with "sit" is that they don't sit when they are supposed to. They sit when it is convenient for them. There is rarely a time that it works for both of you. When a distinguished guest arrives for dinner and your dog jumps up on her evening dress, what happened to "sit"?

To train a good "sit," start with the leash on your dog. Say "sit" then *place your dog* into a sit position. (Do not wait to see if your dog will sit on his own.)

Praise your dog verbally with exuberance, but do not touch him now. If he gets up, quickly fix him back in the "sit" position and say "no, sit" as you correct him. Continually praise him, and notice if exuberant praise will cause him to break his "sit." He must learn to remain sitting during high levels of distraction, so practice this part often.

Release with command "free" or "okay."

Repeat at each doorway inside your home. Progress to doorways exiting your home. If you live in an apartment building, include sitting at elevator doors, from the hallway into the elevator, and from inside the elevator out into the hallway.

Jumping

Jumping has been addressed in other sections of this volume because it is probably the number one complaint of dog owners. Those who are not dog people can generally tolerate a dog that minds its own business, but a dog of any size on their body is considered a very bad thing. It is very, very bad when it is your dog.

Basic causes of jumping include excitement, investigation, and overstimulation.

A possible cure for the jumping that frequently occurs from excitement would be to have the dog's owner knock on their own door prior to entering their home. This greatly reduces the excitement level of the average dog. If he comes to believe that it is just a family member coming home, he will be less apt to go bonkers, believing that it is a novel visitor. Work this sit exercise while someone is knocking on the door and then open the door to enter your home. Keep your dog sitting until he appears calm and well mannered. Release the dog, maintaining leash control to assure his good behavior. Add doorbell rings to the training protocol as your dog becomes "sit" reliable at your front door. This is an impossible exercise without a leash on your dog at first, so don't try to cheat. This exercise will take weeks to perfect. It is well worth the effort.

Building a Good "Off" Command Start by putting the leash on your dog. When your dog jumps up on you, pull the leash gently yet briskly straight up as you say "off." Your dog will oppose the upward leash action and want to go back down toward the floor. Praise your dog exuberantly with "good off" and proceed to creating a "sit" position (with physical placement) while continuing your verbal praise.

When your dog begins to jump on someone else, say "off" as your dog is starting the jump, again leash correct your dog using the leash with a quick corrective motion to the side, not downward. If you pull your dog down, he will struggle to pull up. Pull the leash laterally when your dog is attempting to jump on a visitor. Ask the setup visitor to step back outside the door if your dog so much as looks like he is going to start again and jump. The only way the visitor is coming in, is if your dog maintains his calm behavior. "Sit" is again the eventual outcome. I like the guest to offer a food reward when the dog shows calm, cognitive behavior.

Jumping on furniture and counters can be remedied by remote correction, which was addressed earlier in this chapter.

Special word to those with dogs that only jump when they are off the leash. *Keep the leash on* during all his supervised waking hours, or you will be looking toward remote collar training. You must be able to reinforce what you ask for.

Mounting

Mounting behaviors may look like a dance on the conga line, but the gesture may be one of dominance. Puppies will often mount other puppies in their simultaneous quest for height and social elevation.

Mounting may also be a result of some aberrant sexual behaviors. I have seen dogs that mount anonymous objects, including their beds.

In male dogs neutering tends to reduce this behavior. In female dogs, an increase in mounting behavior may occur after being spayed.

This may be handled as a hormonal issue. Offending individuals should be leash corrected and placed into "down-stay." Daily obedience sessions help you to maintain structural clarity. Dogs that are comfortable with their subordinate position mount less often than dogs with unresolved dominance issues.

Barking

Barking, in terms of nuisance behavior, is up there with jumping. It is even worse if you happen to be the next-door neighbor of a barking dog.

Let's look at a few barking scenarios.

Barking in the crate is treated by covering the crate with an old sheet. Then, while the dog cannot see you, bang the top of the crate to startle him into a state of peace and quiet.

Barking at the door when guests arrive goes back to the doorway behavior, which is sit quietly at the door and wait to be released by the owner.

Barking that results from separation anxiety is addressed by conditioning your dog to be comfortable with being alone (see section on separation anxiety).

Barking in the backyard can be addressed with short supervised trips into the backyard on a lead. While on lead, should your dog inappropriately begin barking, make a leash correction and say "quiet." Offer praise when your dog is clearly quiet with intentions to stay that way. Do not praise too quickly after your dog stops barking. If your dog is even thinking of barking again and you say "good dog," then you asked him to bark. Watch your timing on this one. Praise only a quiet dog that is now giving you focus, instead of the dog that is still considering singing at the party that created the barking in the first place. Do not leave your dog alone in the backyard for endless hours at a time. This is boring and lonely for your dog. You might try feeding your dog outside to show him how nice outside can be for a little while. Only play with him outside in the yard if you want him to enjoy being out there. Give him a hard plastic baby pool in the hot summer months to stay cool. Bring him inside often for contact with your family. Your dog is a member of your family. If he is not, what's going on?

When I was a teenager I flew homing pigeons and visited the

Bronx Pigeon Club after school whenever I could. I often wondered how carrier pigeons in World War I knew how to locate their home. One reason why they returned so easily may have been an issue of training or one of fufillment. Older pigeon fanciers taught me some-thing about fulfillment. Pigeons always drink water after they eat. The birds were fed by hand by the soldier and then released so that they could fly to their home loft to drink their water. Applying a similar strategy may help teach your dog to enjoy the backyard and therefore bark less frequently. If barking is an extreme problem maybe you should only feed him outdoors, or only play with him outside, and generally ignore him inside the house.

"Wait"

"Wait" is a general area term. Your dog may wait in a standing, sitting, or down position. "Wait" is not as absolute as "sit-stay" or "down-stay." If this confuses you, then do not train it into your dog because you will surely confuse him.

Teaching "wait" is done with a leash. As you are walking, ask your dog to wait and check the leash with a slight jerking motion as you stop walking. When your dog turns toward you to see why you yanked the leash, you should praise "good wait," and release with the terms "free" or "okay" and begin to walk again. Repeat these steps until you see your dog stop walking on the "wait" command. Next, try this at a doorway. Ask your dog to wait as you walk through the doorway. If your dog starts to follow, place the dog back into the orig-inal spot and try again. He may move around a bit but should not be permitted to follow you through the doorway. Initially, return quickly to your dog and praise him. Occasionally, you should call your waiting dog through the doorway using your release word.

"Leave It"

"Leave it" means do not pick it up. How many times have you seen a dog owner unsuccessfully attempt to stop their dog from grab-bing a piece of old pizza crust off of the ground? The "leave it" com-mand is used in these instances. This exercise begins with your dog on a slack leash. Corrections are offered in the way of brisk leash correc-tions when applicable. Throw a tissue or other interesting article on the ground as you simultaneously say "leave it." As your dog makes an effort toward the tissue, give him a correction and immediately praise him for leaving it. Repeat this exercise often, using special food treats. When you can call your dog away from food, you are training well. If I throw down a piece of hot dog and say "leave it," I will pick it up and feed it to him as a reward for leaving it when originally commanded.

"Easy" (Teaching a Soft Mouth)

Many dogs are rough with their mouths when they take food or a toy. The "easy" command, sometimes called "gentle" or "nice," is designed to teach your dog to soften its mouth when taking food or objects from your hand.

There are several ways to accomplish this exercise. One technique is to push the food at your dog very fast in order to stimulate his normal reflex to oppose and pull his head slightly back instead of lunging toward the hand offering the treat. Always give the command as you are providing the treat.

I will sometimes use treats that are spreadable, such as cream cheese. A small spread of peanut butter or cream cheese often helps your dog to accept food by licking it out of your hand instead of eating your fingers.

Feeding open handed and allowing your dog to take food from the palm of your hand will eliminate your fingers from being chewed.

Conventional leash corrections may be applied while offering food to an overzealous pooch, but do not create fear of your hand while trying to teach the "easy" command. Take your time and try any or all of the aforementioned techniques.

Mouthy Puppies

Puppies must quickly learn how not to mouth humans. This normal yet highly unacceptable behavior must be consistently discouraged. I use a variety of techniques to discourage mouthy behaviors. One approach is to hide a canister of breath freshener in your hand and when your puppy mouths your hand say "ouch" and spray a bit into his mouth. When he withdraws, exuberant praise is in order to assure that the puppy does not repeat the mouth performance. Another technique I use is to push your finger into his mouth as he brings his mouth to your hand to mouth you. The deeper you push your finger into his mouth, the more likely he will be to gag and withdraw. All along you will maintain a friendly demeanor and praise your dog for withdrawal of his mouth. I should not forget to remind you that conventional leash corrections work well for mouthy behavior too. When using a leash correction for mouthing be sure not to take your hand away from your dog's mouth, wait until the correction takes his mouth away from your hand, and you can stroke him and pat him and he will not dream of biting you. The leash is not holding him back away from biting you, the brisk leash correction makes it clear to your dog that on a slack leash he cannot bite. This technique works well when an adult works the leash and a child pets the dog. Should the dog try to bite at the child, the adult will offer the leash correction.

"Kennel Up"

Training your dog to walk into a crate on command sure beats chasing him throughout your house, yelling at your children to catch him as he speeds past them with a smirk on his face. Having your dog enjoy his crate is a good place to begin. Your dog's crate should have ample space for lying down and be in an area of your home that regularly has family members coming and going.

I generally sit on the floor in front of the crate to begin teaching this exercise. I send the dog to the crate by basically pushing him in and giving the command "kennel up" simultaneously. I offer a great treat and then invite him out. I turn him around and send him in again. I do not wait to see if he is going to go by himself, I just push him in and quickly reward him and invite him back out so that I may repeat the exercise roughly six to eight times. I will repeat this process several times daily. After the exercise is over, I do not leave the dog in the crate.

I separate the exercise of sending the dog to the crate from actually putting the dog in the crate for any long period of time. As always, the crate is never used as a punitive tool. I am not of the mind-set to use the crate for time-out, for I feel that once wrong behavior has been corrected then there is no need for time-out. Train away any problems that you encounter and there will be no need for you to lock up your dog. Time-out only gives you temporary peace, and the original problem will eventually reoccur at a later date.

Demanding Attention

Watch sometime as a young seemingly submissive puppy runs up to an adult dog, rolling on his back while wiggling all over the place. Observe as the adult may growl and bare his teeth. This puppy is too aggressive for the adult. The puppy has the audacity to come over without first gesturing consent from the elder. This is bad, very bad. When you see the puppy roll over, do not assume that is a friendly gesture. Try not to verbally lash the growling adult, because they are more adept at reading body language than you are. Learn from them; I do.

When your dog nuzzles you, it is his way of urging you to stroke him, and it is demanding and often aggressive behavior. I may be a bit conservative here, but I have seen so many dogs of different breeds demand attention one minute and then proceed to bite the very next minute. Ask your dog to do anything at all for you prior to your kind touch. Physical praise should be on your terms, not his. Ask him to sit if you want to stroke him, call him to you, and if he comes, then pet him. If you call your dog to come to you and he doesn't, then do not go to him and praise him anyway. You would be reinforcing his inappropriate behavior.

Dogs are so smart, they kick their empty water bowls around for you to fill them. They scratch at the door to be let out and bark when they want a cookie. Who is the employer here? Do you feed your dog, provide excellent medical coverage, and housing? I think you are the employer. If you water the dog on his demand, walk your dog on his demand, or pet your dog on his demand, then he is the employer. Why would your dog come to you on your command if you are the employee? He would not. Become the big dog for your dog. He will appreciate it, I promise.

Practical Obedience Exercises

"Sit"

I've always said I'd rather have a dog with a great "sit" instead of a dog that sort of knew five commands. A great "sit" makes a well-controlled dog, end of story. You need to build this command into

Sit

your mission because it is the foundation of several levels of control.

The basic premise is that your dog sits instantly on a single command from you. Not quite as basic a premise is that your dog sits instantly, whether he was moving quickly toward a ball or coming up from a lying down position. To top it off, your dog is to sit until released on command "free" or "ready."

When multiple commands are uttered—"sit! sit! sit!! sit, I *said* SIT!"—your dog will learn not to respond to your first command. It would be unfortunate if your voice meant nothing without using extreme tonal inflection or considerable volume. If you use multiple commands your dog will learn to ignore the first few and wait for the loud one. Dogs cannot understand that you mean what you say the first time if you don't make them do it until after the fifth time. Say "sit" once and help your dog to assume this position. When he sits, praise him exuberantly. It is imperative that you work on keeping him in a "sit" position until you release him. When he becomes accustomed to holding the sit position during exuberant praise, you can work it up to his not moving when you throw a ball or put down the dinner dish. Slowly build up the time he has to sit still, and add distractions as he shows responsibility in this position. Three minutes is a nice goal to work toward.

Training Techniques "Sit" is a position your dog will take of his own volition many times daily. It cannot be harmful in any way to name this position (sit) when you notice your dog about to take a seat. Furthermore, it is also okay to reward the dog for taking the position as you name it and praise your dog for assuming it.

When helping your dog to sit, you may push a treat downward and back from just above his head and steer him into a sit, or you can run your hand down his back and gently apply pressure behind his knees, or pull up on his collar until he sits. Go with whatever works and always use the route with least resistance. Reward your dog with verbal praise, a treat, or a vigorous game of tug-of-war.

Try not to push on his back because he will naturally oppose the action. Train him for three to five minutes at a time, and end your session on a glorious note. It is often helpful to crate the dog for a little while after your session so he can unwind.

"Stand"

The "stand" command is helpful in grooming and conformation situations. I find the "stand" command also helps teach puppies not to automatically go from sit to down. They pay more attention to the given command as opposed to performing a patterned exercise.

Teach this by having your dog in a "sit" position. Have a great treat available in your hand and show your dog the back side of the hand with the treat in it and pull it away from his face and say "stand." Encourage him to move forward one step to rise up out of the sitting position. I have trained dogs using a sling type of device under the belly, but the dog does oppose the lifting up of its rear. Most dogs will learn "stand" from one or the other technique.

"Down"

The "down" command is very important, and it has been well published that dogs with a dominance problem will struggle against the position. For a change, I agree that the dogs that fight the "down" position tend to fight in other areas of obedience as well. The exercise begins with the dog sitting. I teach the "down" by using food lures and find most dogs are willing to "down," if the treat works for them. A week or so later, I add a hand signal coupled with physical place-ment by creating a pulley by slipping the slack in the leash under my shoe and pulling up on the line. This is an informational exercise because I want to know who is doing "down" just for food, and who is going to fight the placement. I want to learn which dog is handler compliant versus which dog is handler insensitive or dominant. I'm also trying to figure out how long it will take for your dog to recover if you wrestle him into going down, and how easy or difficult are the repetitions following the initial placement. The hand signal resembles having your hand raised up over your head like in grade school. This is a clear visual cue. Raise and then lower your arm to your side while

Down

teaching the "down." Play games with your dog that have him fly into the down position, perhaps to win the ball or a treat. Speedy "downs" are what we like to see.

To initially teach "down" at a distance, start with the "sit" position. Back approximately six feet away from your dog, and as you take a giant step toward your dog, put your hand up for a signal and gently snap the lead in a downward position. As your dog goes down, step inward and reward with a treat. Increase distance away from your dog until your dog "downs" at any distance. Another way is to tie your dog to a tree on a buckle collar and have a second collar on him with a second training leash attached. He can't walk ahead, so you can command him to "down" from several feet away. If he fails to "down," you can try snapping the lead from where you are standing. If he responds, walk up to him, reward him, then release him. This process can only work on a dog that first understands the "down" command fully with distractions while near the owner, before beginning to slowly increase your distance away from your dog to achieve the same control at greater distances.

Practice getting your dog to go straight to "down" from a "stand" position. Practice the "down" in motion, first walking, then running.

The bottom line is that your dog must obey "down." Have patience but make sure your dog "downs" on one command and stays "down" until released by command. When your dog is clear on what "down" is and that he should "down" anywhere, at any time, at any distance with every conceivable distraction, then he knows "down." Don't short yourself and your dog by cheating on this one. Practice with repetition and positive reinforcement and you will slowly accomplish this level of training.

"Stay"

The "stay" command is the savior for hyperdog syndrome. A correct "stay" may be accomplished in a "sit," "down," or "stand" position. Once the command is given, your dog may not move his feet. If he wants to, he may spin his head around like the devil himself, but he may not move his feet. This lesson is trained in three phases. Phase one is where we teach your dog what "stay" means. We are very close to the dog and always have control of his leash.

Time is the first element of the "stay" command. You can build up slowly to about thirty minutes or so before you advance to the next phase of challenges or distractions. Should your dog attempt to remove himself from the "stay" position prior to being released, physically fix him back into his absolute original position and repeat your command to "stay." Picture a television program where a homicide has occurred and the detective is examining the crime scene. The position of the body is chalked off, indicating where and how it was found. It is not a bad idea whenever possible to chalk off your dog's position while he is in a "stay." If he moves, it will be easy for you to see where he originally was. Release him while he is doing it well, and build the time up slowly over weeks. Roughly speaking, your dog should be able to do a ten-minute "down-stay" after one week of daily practice.

On any given day of the week I may watch an owner give the body language to their dog that says "come" while they are uttering the command "stay." To make matters worse, when the dog breaks his "stay," the owner tries to compensate for the break by saying "come." It is wrong to allow a dog to ignore a "stay" without a correction. You may only release your dog if he is staying put in his place until you say "okay." This security may save his life someday.

Distractions are doled out incrementally once your dog is clear that "stay" means do not budge. Remember, you are still inches from your dog at this point so that you may make timely and effective corrections should your dog try to move before you release him. This phase may also be considered the proofing phase. Wise dog owners proof every command prior to offering responsibility to their dogs. Should a tennis ball roll past your dog while in the "stay" position, can you be certain that your dog will remain quietly in the "stay" position or will he bolt? Is your dog calm or jittery while in the "stay" position? Before you leave him alone in the "stay," proof him with every possible distraction.

Distance is the final element to work with after you have successfully well proofed the "stay" with antagonizing distractions. I begin training distance by placing the dog in a "down-stay" position alongside a wall. I walk just out of sight of the dog with leash still in hand. I am only two feet away but out of the dog's vision. Should the dog move, I can "fix" him back into the "down-stay" and disappear again. I begin distance training in a quiet environment and offer distractions

Stay—front position

Stay—heel position

only after I have built up the time that the dog will successfully "stay" while I am away and out of sight.

I routinely will not call my dog to me from a "stay." I return to him and give him a reward, but the dog waits for me to return and release him.

This is good solid training and as in all good training each element needs to be broken down into small parts so that your dog can understand exactly what you need from him. These exercises will take months of work, so remember rushing will only confuse your dog.

"Heel"

I remember as a kid watching Dick Van Dyke do a routine about someone walking their dog. He acted as though he were attached to the bumper of a car and being dragged by it. Of course there was only an imaginary dog on a leash in the skit, but we all have witnessed this scenario if not actually experienced it.

There is a difference between a formal "heel" and loose-leash walking. "Heel" is the position where the dog's right shoulder is aligned with your left leg. Loose-leash walking allows your dog to walk informally around you but not forge ahead on the leash.

Techniques for Training "Heel" "Heel" is trained by teaching your dog to go to your left leg. Beginning with your dog sitting in front of you, he can get into the "heel" position by curling around your right side to your left leg, or can back his body directly into the "heel" position. When you are not walking, your dog should sit quietly yet attentively at your left side in "heel" position. When you walk forward, your dog should keep pace in "heel" position. If you should take a few steps backward your dog should be doing the same to keep in "heel" position.

Training has to do with teaching your dog how to fix itself every time you move forward and backward, make right turns and left turns, do right-about and left-about turns. If you think this is hard, you are right. This type of training is artistic, athletic, frustrating, and rewarding. Most of my clients are not interested in the finer points of "heel" position and its formalities in the ring. They are more interested in not getting dragged out of doorways and down the street two or

Moving to "heel" position

three times a day, seven days a week, 365 days a year, for the next four-teen or so years.

Loose-Leash Walking With a puppy I begin my leash walking with a lot of high-pitched friendly talk to get his attention frequently. I will reward him with food treats and all kinds of toys for looking at me as we walk along. I keep the distances short at first to make the experience positive for the puppy. I increase the distance only after I teach turns with focus and quick stops and sits. All along, the puppy is being played with and rewarded with food for giving focus and walk-ing along with you. This is a good prerequisite for formal "heel" train-ing as well. This procedure keeps your dog from pulling on the leash away from you. Treats and games are the rewards of focus. Most dogs are very willing to forgo their forging for a tasty treat or a good game of tug. Commands of "let's go" are given when your direction or pace changes.

When your dog forges, you can check the leash with an abrupt yank as you command "easy" or "whoa." Praise him when there is slack on the leash and continue walking. If you find yourself con-stantly checking the leash, then your yanks are not abrupt enough. Make it clear once or twice and be done with it. Gentle yanks are very annoying to dogs. Do not annoy your dog; train him and praise him for the job well done. Be sure the job is well done before you start praising an inappropriate dog.

"Come"

The "come" command is the one that everybody seems most concerned with. This vision of your dog rushing back to you, jumping post and rail fences to get to your side, is charming yet somewhat unrealistic, unless you train well and have a well-fulfilled dog. Those of you who feel that chasing your dog is great fun will have a nightmare on your hands when now trying to teach the "come." Another prob-lem is when you try to quickly grab at your dog to catch him because he came close to you. This backfires because your dog learns to remain just beyond your reach. First, your dog should want to "come." Second, your dog will learn that he must "come" when called. No tricks, bribes, or grabbing at him will result in your dog happily "coming" on command. I promise you that if your dog has the appro-

Moving to "come" position

priate character for your lifestyle, then you will successfully train your dog to "come" when called. Hard work is in your future, but as they say, anything worth having is worth working for.

Initially I reward a dog with food for stepping in my direction when I call "come." One step in my direction will get him his reward. I will shape him into a dog who will sit straight in front of me on the single command to "come." This "sit in front" is actually the end of the "come" exercise, the place where your dog is supposed to show up in the end. Teaching the "sit in front" is done as you take a step back and away from your dog, which enables your dog to get the picture of where he is to move to (between your knees and sit). Early in the training, when I have the dog come to me I feed him as he comes through between my legs. I reward this as a way to help make the dog feel comfortable with coming in very close to me. I remember when training my dog Fred for the recall, I used a tennis ball. I would occasionally put him in a "stay," walk thirty yards, turn, play with the ball as Fred watched anxiously, and then call "Fred come." He ran like a bullet toward me, and as he neared I threw the ball between my legs. He ran, chasing the ball right under my legs doing what seemed like a hundred miles per hour. This exercise kept up his speed on recalls. I shaped the "sit" in front later as an intermittent exercise so as not to slow him down on the recall.

When you have family helpers you can start your dog close to you on a leash, then reward him for his forward motion toward you and have your helper hold him back away from you a few feet. Act in an exuberant playful manner as you call his name several times quickly. When he is straining to get to you, command Fido to "come." This is when the helper frees up the leash and allows your dog to run to you. Run backward as your dog is running to you and he will increase his speed toward you. When he catches up, feed him, praise him "good come," play with him, and then do it again. If you are tired, I mean physically exhausted, then you are training well. If not, then speed everything up to just short of hectic. Hectic is when the dog is no longer accepting commands in a clear fashion. You can recognize this state by your dog's panting, lacking focus, and being jittery in the body as well as the mind. Keep your dog focused on the exercise and learn how to feel the praise level required to insure correct responses.

Once your dog is clear on what "come" is and he comes fast and sits in front of you, it's time to add distractions to your training. Your dog is still on a leash when you begin to add distractions. The leash should be around six feet long. Begin by allowing your dog freedom to sniff around, investigating something or someone interesting. When you call "Fido, come," immediately begin running backward so that he may chase after you. When he catches up to you, reward and play. Repeat this eight to ten times, then end with a strong play session. When you can effectively call your dog away from another dog, then you can begin to increase the length of the line. All along, increase the level of distractions. Perhaps have someone call your dog and show him a ball or a hot dog, and as he runs toward them, call him. Should your dog fail to respond, run backward as you yank at the leash. As he turns toward you, praise him and have him continue to speed to you. When he gets to you, praise and play with him. Shorten your distance the second you see a slow response to the single command to come. Reliability is based on consistent training.

Before you can fulfill your dreams of a reliable off-leash dog, you must follow the steps. Once your dog is 100 percent reliable on a long (fifty- to a hundred-foot) line with great distractions, you can begin your off-lead work.

Off-lead training starts with first dropping your end of the long line and allowing your dog to drag it. We can always pick it up for a quick correction if necessary. The correction at this time will change from you running backward to you walking on the line, actually stepping on the dragline, and walking up toward your dog. Take the lead about three feet away from his collar and command "Fido, come" and check his leash toward you as you back up. Repeat this as you step back and command your dog to come. Praise him with every step he takes toward you. Even though you are physically correcting him, you must praise him with each step he takes in your direction. When you have stepped back all the way to where you were when you first called him, give him lavish praise and send him out again on the dragline and start again.

Go to "Place"

"Place" is the command used as a grounding spot for your dog. If you point to a spot in the corner of a room, your dog should go there and "down" until further notice. He should get comfortable and not move. This is a nice control command and can be very useful when visitors are afraid of dogs. "Place" allows the dog to remain in the room, just doing "down" in the corner of the room, out of the way, as well-behaved dogs should.

Teaching the "place" is easy. I begin by throwing a hot dog or toy into a corner, and as the dog runs for it I say "place." I make a game out of showing the dog where I am about to throw the item, and as I throw, I command "place." I put the dog in a "sit-stay" and walk to the corner where I drop the reward. Then, I go back to the dog and release him with a "place" command and watch him run into the corner. Next I send him into the area with a "place" command, then give a "down" command, then reward and quick release from the "down." I extend the "down" in "place" slowly over time. I like to define the place spot by using a mat or bed whenever possible. I find this makes the training a bit easier.

Dogs that resist are put back on the long house lead, physically taken on command to the "place" spot, and given a "down" command. Compliance is essential to the reward and release.

Advanced Exercises

If there was such a thing as a good chronic disease, training would be it. The more you train, the more you will want to train. The better your dog responds to you, the better your overall relationship will be. Training is goal oriented so that there is always something new and fun as well as challenging and rewarding to learn.

In-Motion Exercises

Training exercises, even the basic ones, should be advanced to where you can give your moving dog a command and receive an immediate response. Imagine your dog running away from you toward a group of stray dogs, and when you command "down," he drops to the ground like a sack of potatoes. This instant in-motion "down" could save your dog's life. Should your dog be running for trouble, you can secure him with an instant "sit," "stand," "down," or "come."

Training in-motion exercises begins with your dog on a leash. Your pace is slow to moderate, with your dog walking on your left in heel position. If you are teaching an in-motion "sit," then say "sit" and simultaneously check the lead, and if necessary, position the rump into a "sit." Step ahead one or two paces with the leash still in hand and step back into heel position. Should your dog try to rise up, fix the sit and try again to walk ahead one or two steps. When you can, step ahead, then return back to your dog as he maintains the "sit" position. Release your dog, play for a minute, and repeat the exercise. You are doing well when you can walk at a normal pace, command "sit," drop your leash, and continue walking with your dog sitting exactly where you said "sit." Your dog should be waiting for you to call him or waiting for you to return to him. Progression from this point is when you increase your walking speed, until you can run and have the same quick "sit" response as you had walking.

Once the "sit" is clear you can begin training the "down" or "stand" positions. It helps to train yourself to give each command at a certain vocal pitch so it is easier for the dog to discern "sit" from "down" from "stand," etc. Keep the pitch of each command consistent, and your dog will learn the in-motion exercises quickly.

Teaching Retrieve

Teaching your dog to pick up things in his mouth such as the daily newspaper is not too difficult an exercise for your dog to learn. It begins by showing your dog how to target the area that you point to with your finger. Throw small bits of food on the ground as you say "take it." Once your dog understands that he should search the floor for whatever you dropped because he may earn a reward, throw a piece of food on the floor and say "take it." As your dog tracks this piece of food, secretly drop another behind your back. Then, command your dog to "take it." Try to sneak several pieces of food to the floor and point to each and direct him to "take it." You should intermittently throw a ball or favored toy for your dog and send him to "take it," in much the same way as you sent him to take the food. When he brings the ball, take the ball from his mouth, saying "drop." As you take it from your dog, offer him a food reward from your hand. Show the dog slowly and quietly to take objects that you present. If you get resistance, gently pry your dog's mouth open and place the object in his mouth. Command him to "hold" it as you tap his lower jaw to help him be successful with holding it. Command "drop" and allow him to drop it into your hand, then reward him with a treat or game of tug.

This exercise can first be trained as a game. Throw a ball or toy out for your dog to retrieve. When your dog goes out for it, take a second ball or a second toy and call your dog, showing him the one you have in your hand. Dogs seem to always want the one you have in your hand instead of the one they have in their mouths, so when your dog sees and wants the article you have, command "drop," and when he drops, throw the second one away from you in the opposite direction that you threw the first article. When your dog runs to the second article thrown, pick up the first article dropped and get ready to show it to your dog as he comes running back toward you. Command "drop" and when he does, throw the article in your hand with the command "take it."

The point here is that you are not actually taking away anything from your dog but replacing the article. In a short time, your dog will be running out to "take" and quickly returning to you for the "drop" and for another "take it." This exercise is great fun and offers you excellent control.

In situations where you are out walking your dog and he finds a piece of old pizza crust that he will not drop, first give the "drop" command, then taking hold of his buckle collar, lift his front feet up about two inches off the ground and hold him up there until he figures out that it is easier to move air through his lungs if he drops something out of his mouth. When he drops the food or whatever out of his mouth, lower him to the ground and praise him "good drop." You are not hanging him up to choke him to death; you are teaching him to relinquish articles from his mouth. Dogs that fail to drop from the mouth are not safe walking on city streets. The uncomfortable feelings that you will have lifting your dog up this way should be offset by the possibilities of your dog having abdominal surgery to remove foreign objects from his body.

Competition Training

I used to believe that competition training was useless. I had this notion that the dog who was perfect in the ring might be horrendous outside, where obedience really mattered. In fact, I made many house calls where ribbons and trophies were displayed proudly on the mantel, but the dogs had serious behavioral problems.

In my own training, I had been taught that club trainers were less skilled than private in-home trainers, and that competition-style training exercises were fun to do but ineffective in terms of "real" obedience. I learned later that although it is possible to have a ring-wise dog who performs the moves in the obedience ring only, the competition exercises could in fact be used functionally.

Being a dog guy and being interested in everything everybody has to say about dogs, I listened to my friend Sue Sternberg. Sue suggested that even if you do not want to compete your dog in obedience, the chosen exercises in American Kennel Club obedience competitions are fun and challenging. When a trainer is training for a high score in competition, every move must be correct. Sue asked me, "As a trainer, shouldn't you be interested in the most correct postures and positions each exercise offers?" The answer was, of course, yes. Although you may fall a bit short of perfect in your own ability to teach, if your trainer is goal oriented, at least you are attempting to strive for the perfect dog. If your trainer counsels you improperly, you will probably find your team (you and your dog) falling way short of your intended goal.

I am forever grateful to my friend Gisela Engel for introducing me to Michael and Linda Zenobia, German shepherd dog breeders and importers who showed me the road to Schutzhund sport. Schutzhund was developed in Germany as a tool to test the temperament of German shepherd dogs, and prior to breeding, the dog must pass this test, which insures that shepherds with weak characters will not be bred. This test has evolved into a competition dog sport over the years and is now a three-phase competition that consists of tracking, obedience, and protection. Because of the strict obedience and tracking exams used in Schutzhund, the title "Schutzhund (Protection Dog)" might be better renamed so as not to have the general public believe that the dogs competing in Schutzhund are aggressive animals. Michael Zenobia calls the three phases Obedience, Obedience, Obedience! He says that a dog will not track a scent when commanded to if he is not obedient. In the protection phase, a dog will not go out and bite, and then release his bite on command, if not obedient. The obedience portion of the sport is also difficult and challenging. A dog cannot pass this test if there is an obvious lack of control. Grandfather to the German shepherd dog, Max von Stephanitz, the man credited for the development of this breed, felt that a good dog has the concentration to track a scent, the compliance to perform obedience for his owner, and the courage to protect his home and family, but only when necessary.

Schutzhund sport is not for every dog. If you have a terrier, then there is a sport for your dog, and it has to do with hunting varmints. Owners of breeds not entirely suited for Schutzhund competition may pick out exercises that interest them and train their dogs in this fashion, or choose the exercises of another dog sport.

Any dog can compete in American Kennel Club obedience, and I urge you to look into it so that you can train your dog to be all that he can be. Competition training will keep you and your dog from becoming bored with the routine exercises over and over again.

The United Schutzhund Clubs of America may be reached at the following address:

United Schutzund Clubs of America
3810 Paule Avenue
St. Louis, MO 63125-1718
www.germanshepherddog.com

Others may contact the American Kennel Club for the rules and regulations pertaining to American Kennel Club competition activities.

The American Kennel Club
51 Madison Avenue
New York, NY 10010
www.akc.org

Professional Dog Training

There are times when reading books just does not cut the mustard. People know when that time has come because they have tried with all manner of books and articles and still have problems. There is no shame in seeking out an expert when you are having problems with the behavior of your dog. Most experts would agree that owners, in their quest to do the right thing, often do the opposite. We would rather have the chance to address problems as soon as they are noticed. The greatest chance of success is with a new behavior, not one that has somehow been reinforced for a period of time. Behavior is similar to dermatology in that if it took three months for skin to look bad with no treatment, then it will take six months to recover skin with proper treatment. Remember this little pearl of wisdom next time you let a problem behavior pass you by with no training. If you need help, find a dog trainer.

Where to Find a Qualified Dog Trainer

My first and best advice here is to ask your dog's veterinarian. I am not swearing that every veterinarian is skilled at choosing a dog trainer but at least he will be honest with you, and if he trusts a trainer well enough to refer you to him, try the recommendation.

Ask people on the street with well-trained dogs where they have gone. Ask dog groomers and breeders for recommendations. Breed clubs often have trainers associated with their clubs, so this is usually a sound resource.

When you talk to a professional, he will not offer you a guarantee because life has too many twists and turns for anyone to give guarantees. I can hardly guarantee my very own actions from one day to the next. How can I possibly guarantee that although I teach you a behavior to in turn teach your dog, that you will do it just as I said it should be done, and then furthermore guarantee that the dog will fulfill the behavior every time? Sounds impossible because it *is* close to impossible. Dogs learn well with consistency, and that is what a good dog trainer should provide you, consistency. If Rover is making progress then that is a positive sign that Rover is learning, so if your trainer is progressing with your dog, move along and keep training.

Private trainers who visit the home are a convenient way for your family and dog to be educated. Search for a reliable trainer and look for the trainer's abilities to teach you what has to be done. If your dog only listens to your dog trainer, what happens when he goes home? If at every lesson your trainer handles your dog, I hope you are taking notes because you may have a problem if your trainer goes out of town. You must handle your own dog. Guidance is great, but you, the owner, must, as they say, walk the walk. We demand it of the dog, so why should we be allowed to demand less of ourselves.

Puppy kindergarten classes are fun and informative while providing your puppy with a social atmosphere in which to learn and grow within the structure. I love to watch the puppies after class; they have great fun and learn how to respond to their owners during this play period. Puppy classes should always be structured toward positive reinforcement.

Trainers who are violent and punitive should be avoided. Be clear that negative reinforcement is a good tool for training dogs, but beating a dog is cruelty, not negative reinforcement. I heard of a case where a so-called dog trainer hung up a Sheltie in a class setting for barking too much. This nasty man had a device in his training facility to help winch the dogs up in the air in order to hang them. He ultimately killed a dog that he claimed tried to bite him, but the autopsy confirmed multiple beatings, and the man went to jail. Cruelty is never called for in dog training, and if your dog has the type of problem that is not manageable, euthanasia is a far better choice than cruel and inhumane treatment. Whenever possible, dogs with sound character should be rehomed. Euthanasia is only considered as a last resort, when every other alternative has been exhausted.

7.

Dogs and the Family

It's a beautiful sight to watch a child play with the family dog. There can be few pairs as wonderful as a dog and a child who have a terrific relationship. I could go on and on with stories about dogs and kids. Most are the warmest and most gratifying of experiences, while others are not so pleasing. It is important to examine your situation prior to welcoming a new member to your family.

Building the Family Relationship

Dogs are bright enough to structure themselves into your family in a matter of minutes. They can feel their way into the right spot for themselves, taking any comfortable position available. This position that your dog is searching for should clearly be marked for him by your family. I see so many dogs that have effectively positioned themselves between the spouses or between the parents and children when the correct position for your pet dog is the bottom spot, last on line, end of the road.

We like to hope that our children will be so thrilled to finally have a dog after all the time taken to research the breeds, find a quality breeder, and/or search every shelter for the perfect partner, that they will be happy to partake in all the responsibilities as well. Children must be responsible for the care and feeding of the family dog in an effort to show care-giving behavior to the dog, thus physically showing the dog where to obtain drive fulfillment as well as letting him know who's the boss.

Training the dog should be practiced by the children too. Even kids who are four and five years old can train your dog, they just need a little help with the leash work. I find that kids might be better at giving warm and genuine praise than their parents in many cases. Dogs will sometimes work more effectively for kids than for adults. There are many possible reasons for this, one being that strong dogs feel no threat from children, so they readily comply to their commands. Another reason that a dog might respond better to a child is that children are generally very clear about what it is they want, while adults often assume that their dog understands a signal and is just being stubborn and spiteful. Kids are often good teachers to those who know less than they do. Let your child spend time playing with and training your family dog.

Parents' Job

Parents often complain about the lack of responsibility shown by their children when it comes to caring for the family dog. Housewives in particular phone me with their tales of how the family made this decision to obtain a dog and then it becomes Mom's job entirely. Dad comes home from work and he is too tired to take the dog out for a nice evening run. Kids say they would love to play with the dog but all those afterschool activities get in the way, and then there's all that homework. I bet your kids would rather play with their dog instead of doing their homework, if you allowed them to. Mom, this is the truth, and I hope you love dogs because you are about to become very close to one.

I have also had many children contact me with their dog's serious behavioral problems when it should have been a responsible adult placing the call.

Children's Involvement

Children benefit from the discipline of dog ownership. I believe it helps create responsibility. If we do not teach this to our children, then where are they going to learn it? Perhaps teaching our kids to responsibly care for a pet dog will spill into their lives and make them better parents someday. I wonder if it would do a little something to lower the divorce rate too. Responsibility is a discipline, and I hope that as parents you can effectively teach the concepts to your children.

Children must share in the work and can as long as they are physically able to manage the dog. Do not give a six-year-old kid a three-year-old Lab to walk down a city street. If you own a seventy-pound dog and your kid is forty-five pounds soaking wet, what were you thinking about? Kids can't be responsible for dogs that can drag them down helplessly to the ground. Kids *can* feed dogs of all sizes, let them out into fenced areas, play ball with them, brush them, spend quiet time with them, and even walk them, providing that they can manage the size and strength of their dog. Allowing your child to accompany you to the veterinary office when your dog needs a routine examination is suggested. Kids who feel that they can be part of their dog's health care also tend to take more overall responsibility.

Making Introductions

Introducing Puppies to Children

Puppies should be introduced to children as soon as possible. Puppies that are three, four, and five months of age need this exposure, training, and reinforcement to insure proper behavior around children.

Children should be counseled to be calm around puppies. Children should not run very fast or flail their hands around the puppy's face. Parents should supervise their children around dogs until such time that it appears there will be harmony, which may take a while to obtain. Do not just put your kid on the floor like it was some sort of gift for the dog because I have seen dogs aggressively jump on children when this approach was taken. If the dog we are introducing is a puppy, then have the pup on a leash when introductions are in order. In this way, you will have control. Children should be sitting so that we can walk the puppy to the child, as opposed to the child walking up to the pup. Puppies are normally mouthy. Children need to know that before they attempt to touch the puppy. Kids that stretch out their hand and then quickly retract it the second the puppy lifts his head toward their hand are instigating the bite behavior and will quickly teach the puppy that biting works. Once a puppy learns to believe that biting works, and through biting he can fight to win his way, then we have a problem. A potentially big problem. Children must be taught how to handle a puppy by their parents, who are in charge of the lessons. If necessary, the dog and child will only have exposure to each other in small doses. Often it is the active child that promotes this dose approach, not the dog or the dog's behavior. Better to take your time with this building of a long-lasting relationship than just throw it together and hope for the best. Puppies should receive affection and attention in the presence of the children, more so than in the absence of the children. This will help the pup associate the presence of children with affection, attention, and food. Have you ever noticed that dogs that hover under high chairs often like the kids that are hurling food down to them?

Introducing Adult Dogs to Children

When we are introducing a new adult dog, I like to have him in a wire crate so that I can have the dog see the child without the dog having to worry about being grabbed. Should the dog show interest in the child and the child is old enough to listen to instructions, I have the child go to the crate several times and feed the dog some treats. I am leery of a dog that would not normally guard a crate but does so when a child approaches. I might try having the adult dog on a leash for the initial introduction, but any slight tension on the lead might increase the likelihood of the dog becoming defensive. It is common for novice handlers to tense up on a leash and create this defensive behavior. Seasoned handlers have more confidence in their ability to read their dog's actions and prevent any such occurrences. This is why I prefer the crate technique. The crate should not be a stranger to the dog before you make introductions because the dog may begin to associate the child with confinement and therefore be hostile toward children. Dogs should always be intermittently placed into their crates simply as an exercise in good behavior. Dogs should be placed into their crates about an hour before the arrival of children used in the conditioning program. Children should be nonconfrontational (do not let them stand straight in front of a dog, looking eye to eye) and walk toward the crate with smiles on their faces and off to the side a bit as they throw a treat or two into the crate. Having someone stand sideways or on the same side of the dog is much easier for the dog to accept because this is a less threatening posture.

Dogs with high play drive can be swayed toward liking boys who can throw tennis balls all day. Lapdogs seem to enjoy little girls a lot. I can't tell you how many dogs I've seen in strollers being pushed around by three- and four-year-olds.

Pregnant Owners with an Existing Dog in the Home

Hopefully you have a dog that already enjoys kids. Hopefully you know this because your friends have kids that your dog adores. Dogs that have had exposure to children when they were pups have an easier time with this than those who had little or no exposure. No matter, at this time you are going to actively generate good will toward children.

Let me talk to you first-time parents about how it is going to be in the beginning of parenthood. When you have that beautiful bundle and want to go home to relax after the trauma of childbirth, everybody you ever knew will be coming by to see this miracle and bring you presents and diapers. Try to conceive of the kind of tumult I'm talking about, and then consider how your dog is going to feel. Typically, when the baby is in your hands, you tell the dog to go away and lie down. Then, when the baby is asleep, you tell your dog how sorry you are for not having more time for him (who was once "your baby") and lavish him with attention, affection, and kind soothing words. From the dog's perspective, this type of scenario looks like this: when the baby is around I get cut out, when the baby is not around I get it all. Okay then, why should your dog now enjoy the presence of your baby? The reality of this situation is that it will be impossible to give your dog the same amount of affection after your baby is born. Months before the arrival of your baby phase out the amount of attention your dog receives normally, so that it will be easy for him to accept this new baby. Attention, affection, and food are three very important needs that a dog strives to fulfill for itself. Once you teach your dog that these needs are satisfied around your baby, you will find your dog becoming excited at the very sight of the child. Excitement may be in and of itself both good and bad. Do not incite hectic and out-of-control behavior by revving your dog up at the sight of the child, or your dog may try to jump on the baby instead of lying quietly nearby.

Prior to the eighth month, I send my pregnant clients out to buy a doll that cries, flails its arms, and wets. I ask them to try to get a receiving blanket from a friend or from a Lamaze class and wrap the doll with it. I have my clients treat the doll as they would a baby, including walks with a stroller, in order to show the dog how to walk along the stroller in a well-mannered way.

Before your baby is born, borrow diapers from a friend's baby to prepare your dog for the new odors associated with newborn babies.

I have had dog owners buy dolls and treat the dolls like real babies. I ask the client to powder the doll with baby powder and use real diapers just to introduce the scent to their unsuspecting dogs.

Most dogs tolerate the presence of infants. I have only rarely seen dogs attempt to jump into cribs or playpens to try to do harm to infants. One could take a position that an overzealous prey instinct can stimulate a dog to bite an infant. This may be true, but if I see this behavior, the dog is rehomed to where it will not have contact with small children.

When Rover Gets Old

This part of dog ownership is most difficult. Unfortunately dogs just do not live as long as we want them to. Children as well as adults suffer a great emotional loss when their dog dies.

I strongly feel that whenever possible, children should know the truth about what happens to their dog when it goes off to the veterinarian and does not return. Imagine what your child will think of the veterinarian if they believe that the animal doctor did not save their dog. I have seen grown adults who are normally rational individuals became very defensive with the veterinarian when their dogs became ill. Once again, imagine how difficult sickness or eventual death of a pet is to your children. A member of your family is gone.

Parents, you do not have to run out and replace your dog. The place deep in your heart for your dog will always be there. You will find space in your heart for another. The time lapse between losing a dog and obtaining another should depend on how long it takes for you to no longer compare the previous and surely great dog to any new and probably rough-around-the-edges pooch.

When Rover Must Find a New Home

Occasionally a dog just does not work out, no matter how hard you try. Aggression, destruction, and elimination problems lead the list of reasons why dogs should be rehomed.

Kids have a hard time understanding the safety factors involved. I had one young boy tell me he would rather his little brother be rehomed instead of his dog. This is a sticky subject. Children learn by example, so we must watch what we say and what we do. Parents who strike dogs raise children who strike dogs. The same holds true for raising a voice toward the dog. Children can mistakenly feel that if their parents can give away the dog who "was bad" perhaps they too will be given away if they don't behave. It is important to explain any problems the family is having with the dog and try your best to have the children at least hear what concerns may govern the rehoming of the family dog. Kids usually do not go along with the plan, but you as the grown-up have to understand that. The bottom line is that if your dog is a danger to children, he must be rehomed. If your dog is a danger to humans he should be responsibly managed or euthanized.

*   *   *

In general the combination of kids and dogs is usually fantastic when you have the right set of circumstances. First and most important is that the family as a whole has agreed to share the responsibility. Next, the dog must be of sound character and friendly to children. That is it. No huge secrets. Do it and enjoy, you will be busy. The best kind of busy there is.

8.

Multiple-Pet Households

Owning Two Dogs at One Time

I imagine that if you asked a dog if he would enjoy the company of another dog, the answer would be yes. They have lots of fun with each other, and it seems that your dog hardly plays with you in quite the same way. Actually, living with two dogs at a time can be greatly rewarding for all concerned, but be warned it is more than twice the work. I say this because each dog needs his own time for attention and affection separate and apart from his housemate. Walking two dogs on a leash is fine when they each understand how to walk nicely. Being dragged down the street on your belly by two dogs who are trying to savage your neighbor's Yorkshire terrier is not a good thing. You might have to feed them at separate times because dogs often need to be separated when eating to avoid conflict and fighting over the food. Twice

the veterinary, food, and toy expenses per year alone is a good reason to strongly look at owning two dogs. The size of the home will also dictate the breed choices in a multiple situation. Two Yorkshire terriers in a New York City apartment may work out just fine, while two Irish setters may not do as well.

Puppies that spend their first months largely in the company of other dogs may have a big problem focusing on people. This is very important for you to keep in mind. I see many pups that were initially kept by a breeder to see how the pup would develop around many other dogs. When finally placed into a home, they are often not very social toward humans. Owners cannot understand why the pup is so standoffish with them, yet when the pup sees other dogs, it goes ballistic with joy. The point here is that if you get two pups at the same time, you are running the risk of having two dogs that are more interested in each other than in you, the human owner.

Same Breed/Different Breed

Over the years I have noticed that certain breeds seem to come in multiples. Interesting how many Yorkie owners have more than one Yorkie at a time. I have seen this tendency with small and large breeds. The issue to you, the prospective multi-dog owner, is only a question of what you want. Owners contemplating another dog should do so for themselves, not their existing dog. Dogs usually enjoy the presence of another dog yet it must really be an owner's wish for another mouth to feed, body to exercise, and vet bills to deal with. Because of selective breeding, herding dogs have a natural instinct to behave in a particular way. I think two breeds from the same group (herding, for example) may play better together than a herding breed and a toy breed. I have seen a few "odd couples" work out well, too, but I might tend to stay with the group I chose in the first place and have two dogs of perhaps the same group, if not the same breed.

Not forgetting mixed breeds, I then consider the size and weight of my existing dog and try to find a partner to match within a few pounds or a couple of inches.

Same Sex/Opposite Sex

A male and a female statistically have the best chance of getting along well. It is more likely that two females will get along better together than two males, yet I have seen countless males get along well with other male dogs. I have seen male littermates that grow up in the same household get along well, but when maturity hits, they fight with intent to do serious harm to each other. I have had similar experiences with two females. I have seen both male dogs and female dogs fare well with housemates of no relation as well. Females that are gonadally intact may show an increase in aggression prior to and/or during estrus (heat cycle). Males do not have heat cycles and are prepared to breed any standing female in heat at any time of the year. If you are going to keep dogs of both genders around, one or both should be fixed, unless you plan on breeding them.

The bottom line here is that one of each sex tends to be the least problematic. This factor overrides even a sibling relationship. So keep this in mind when considering adding a dog.

Old Dog/Young Dog

Imagine how your old dog feels when jumped by a puppy in the park. First of all, if he has any health problems, like arthritis, being jumped on is not only degrading, it's painful. Most adult dogs run away at the sight of a puppy. I have seen huge rottweilers run from miniature schnauzer puppies, and rightfully so because puppies are crazy with energy. On the other hand, I have witnessed older dogs being rejuvenated by the arrival of a new puppy in the family.

Should a new puppy come into your lives, both you and your older dog need not suffer for it. You can actually have fun with it, if you exercise a little control. I hate using the word control so often, but someone must have the authority to teach and have gained respect for compliance to be achieved. Do not let the new puppy muscle your old dog. Do not allow your old dog to overdominate your new puppy either. Folks, ying and yang, balance is the key to life.

Big Dog/Little Dog

Animal hospitals abbreviate these dog fights as BD/LD. Big dog, little dog, and these are the most devastating events because although it is rare that a dog means to kill another dog, it happens all too often when there is such a size difference. But I have seen many large and small dogs live together in perfect peace, and it is adorable to see. Should you go for this combination be sure not to get a high-energy large dog to live with a fragile timid small dog. Personalities are what we should be matching here. This is the more important issue.

Owning More Than Two Dogs

With the arrival of every new dog, the complexity of the situation increases. The dynamics of the pack structure fluctuates constantly, almost daily. A great example of this is often seen by those who live in multiple-dog households when a subordinate dog finds a bone or some other article. When this subordinate lies down to chew his prize and the dominant dog arrives and wants the subordinate's prize, the subordinate may not give it up and growl, stare, and show its teeth to the dominant dog. Often the dominant dog will just go away and leave the subordinate with the bone. In this case, although we may clearly know who is dominant and who is subordinate, the subordinate is the dominant dog for now. Many factors influence dominance-status events such as hunger and proximity of the dogs to the article. The structure will change within certain parameters. I have seen female dogs be the dominant member of multiple-dog households even though it is usually a male dog's job.

I have found small colonies of dogs to be very pleasant when the owners were responsible and there was enough physical space for them to have a quiet place when necessary. I once visited a horse farm that housed two colonies of dogs. The two breeds housed on this farm were Jack Russell terriers and rottweilers. The Jacks ran the show on this property. The rottweilers clearly had respect for these tenacious little dogs. On another occasion, I saw a Jack Russell bite into the Achilles tendon of an adult German shepherd dog. It was incredibly difficult to remove this little tyrant from the leg of the shepherd. The shepherd just howled in pain and spun around in an attempt to dislodge the Jack. I finally was able to remove the little hellion by prying her mouth open.

My advice for anyone considering owning multiple dogs is to try volunteering at a local animal shelter first so that you can become accustomed to the natural behavior of dogs in pack situations.

It is also helpful to remember that when introducing a new dog to an existing group, leash control is important and whenever possible, remove any objects that can cause possesive acts of aggression. It is also helpful when introducing a new dog to a household to make initial introductions in a neutral area so that you can offset any territorial issues.

Health Considerations in
Multiple-Dog Households

Veterinary expenses are generally reasonable when you only have to deal with routine care. The problem with multiple-dog situations is that when one dog becomes ill with a contagious disease, they all get it. One such condition, an upper respiratory infection called kennel cough, is highly contagious and runs rampant in all too many boarding, training, and even breeding kennels. There is a vaccine for dogs who visit kennels and/or dog shows that helps prevent many strains of the upper respiratory illness. Should your dog come down with it, thank the Lord that it is treatable but nonetheless a pain in the neck. Internal and external parasites are passed between dogs as well. In fact, some parasites may even be passed between dogs and cats.

It is considerably more difficult trying to keep a convalescing dog quiet when his pack is running wild around him. I have been exposed to dogs with delayed fracture healing just because the owners could not keep their dog quiet because of the presence of other dogs in the home. Here is an example of how control in respect to training is helpful in achieving and maintaining good health practices.

Training Considerations in Multiple-Dog Households

Dogs living in pairs, trios, or larger colonies all need to have a special relationship with their human family. I say special because in order for the humans to have control of the environment some form of training is needed. This training should be done with one dog at a time until the relationship is solid and clear. Although it is fine for the dogs to be with one another for scheduled play sessions during the day, it is far more important for each dog to have private time with the family for bonding and training. Once you have good control of your pack, then you can begin to expand on the time that they spend together. Block out a little training time every week for training your group. Keep them sharp in obedience, whether it is one-on-one or the whole group.

Generally, your dog's name would only precede an in-motion command such as "let's go" or "heel." Stationary commands such as "sit" usually do not call for your dog's name prior to the command. But in a multiple-dog setting, it is helpful always to use each dog's name so that each one may be controlled without confusion. If you lined them up in a "sit-stay" and called just one, the others should remain in the "sit-stay." If even one began to move you'd make an ugh-ugh sound followed by the command "Fluffy, staaaaaay."

Your Part in the Hierarchy

How do people really keep numerous dogs *and* maintain peace and harmony? It's an attitude, a learned way to behave around dogs. I know that some owners just have "it," but their numbers are much lower than most people think. The owners that I know who define alpha have a quiet, calm, yet very strong attitude combined with a sense of fairness and compassion that earns them the trust of their dog. Some things come faster for some than for others, but the more contact with dogs that you have had the better you will be. Learning how to read the structure is one imperative component for success. You are calling the shots, but beyond that it is crucial for you to support the hierarchy as it naturally falls. You can't choose who is in charge for them, they must do it, and hopefully without violence.

There are cases upon cases of dog owners who report that their dogs get along fine by themselves, but problems develop when the owner comes home. This is a clear indication that the owners are disrupting the natural order and the subordinate dog is owner-reinforced to be dominant. The way to avoid these problems is to side with the dominant dog and help the subordinate to become comfortable in that space. Realistically, it is more natural for us to yell at the growling dog than it is to yell at the dog that is being growled at. This is wrong. We should side with the dominant dog to try to avoid a fight. If you discipline the subordinate as the dominant dog does then things will change. A common fight scenario is who may greet a visitor first. The dominant dog is allowed to greet first. If the subordinate should be so bold as to try to get to the door first, the dominant dog might attack. Help this situation out by teaching the subordinate to hang back when someone comes in. On a natural level, the dominant dog will allow the subordinate access to the visitor, but in his own time, and the subordinate should wait and look to him for that time.

Trying to help an old dog to be dominant because he came first is not going to work. I have seen small dogs be dominant over big dogs and that is fine, so long as the big dog is okay with that. If the big dog grows up and says enough, then you have to turn it around or the small dog is history. That is hard when the small dog is Pierre, your ten-year-old poodle, and he is being muscled all of a sudden by his brother Rambo, the two-year-old German shepherd dog. When Rambo was a pain-in-the-butt puppy, Pierre used to put him in his place and Rambo would chill out and relax. That behavior lasted until now, when at two years of age Rambo is growling back when Pierre growls at him. Disciplining Rambo might give Pierre temporary safety, but what happens if you leave the house? Time to get on Rambo's side. Hard, huh? If you are correctly reinforcing the hierarchy you should be paying attention to who eats first and best, and the body language that is suggestive of who is the CEO of the company pack.

I do not want to underestimate your power as alpha here. You should always feel as though you can obtain a compliant response when you call for it from any of your dogs. Apart from you, though, there exists a separate and definitive dog-to-dog relationship whenever you have more than one dog. Be alpha but recognize how it trickles down from the top. Learn the dynamics of the structure and don't just focus on your position or perspective. People who understand this have fewer problems overall with multiple-dog households.

I recommend the multiple-pet household to all those who can handle the action. It is wonderful to have a house full of pets that live harmoniously in peace. The responsibility is a great one but a rewarding one all the way down the path.

Minimizing Risk
When Introducing Dogs

This tricky situation should be done on neutral territory so that neither dog feels ownership. If it is apparent that the dogs will play, then great. If we are attempting to get two dogs together and they want to fight, then we are looking at muzzles. I have had numerous cases where after a few weeks of the dogs wearing basket muzzles, they worked out the structure and their muzzles were removed. From this point on, all went well. When using a muzzle, it is important to use one that doesn't prohibit your dog from opening his mouth. This would only frustrate him and cause him to shut down emotionally. What you are looking for is to allow your dog to emotionalize so that we may see how he is reacting to the other dog. Masking the dog's feelings will not allow us to know if they are hostile or friendly. You should never run your dog in the park with a muzzle because if a dog attacks your dog he wouldn't be able to defend himself. In dealing with other dogs you should use muzzles only when trying to get two dogs together.

I feel strongly that dogs do not have to get along with each other.

Humans feel as though it is okay if they can pick and choose their friends but that all dogs must get along. I don't think so. In most major cities today, dogs may run free only in designated outdoor runs. This actually forces dog owners to abandon areas where their dog would be less likely to run into another dog. Many dogs, perhaps even most, enjoy the company of other dogs, but you may have to get used to getting through a fight or two. Choices are: keep your dog on a leash and away from other dogs and, whenever possible, socialize your dog well enough for him to be accepting of other dogs, or run your dog in a traffic-safe environment with a fence so that he can freely exercise without danger of a confrontation.

Minimizing Risk During a Dogfight

If you should find yourself in the middle of a dogfight, you need to assess your situation. Dogs of similar size and weight may only fight for a short time in an attempt to resolve structural hierarchy. At least when dogs of similar size fight, there is a lesser chance of a devastating injury. Do not put your hands or legs into the middle of a dogfight. I have been bitten myself trying to break up fights. At this point, unless I fear a large dog is going to kill a small dog, I will not risk getting my fingers torn off. Cold water from a hose or a bucket often works well. Whenever possible, if you try to run away from a dogfight then you should find that the dogs are less willing to continue fighting. Your dog in the heat of a fight would expect you, a pack member, to enter the fray on his behalf. Standing around and screaming only helps to escalate the commotion. If your dog is on a leash and he gets attacked by a dog with no owner in sight, and if you can't scare the offending dog away, you may find yourself forced to drop your dog's leash to allow him to defend himself. This is in no way an offering from you to encourage a dogfight—this is a matter of respecting your dog's health.

Imagine that if you try to pull your dog's head away from the dog that was actively biting at him. This would create conflict. In your dog's mind, you both should be ganging up on the other dog. I know that your intention is to keep the stray dog away, but that probably will

not happen. A dog intent on attacking your dog will chase him anywhere you move your leash. I know it will be uncomfortable to drop
the leash, but you may not have any better options. Try to find help or
a way to make tremendous noise, such as blowing a whistle or bang-
ing a garbage can cover in order to scare the intruding dog away.

Cats and Dogs

The keys to successful canine and feline relationships have much to do
with the individual pets. Generally, I have found it easy to introduce a
young, somewhat tame, kitten to an adult dog. When kittens are afraid,
they hiss and spit, which usually will spark up a reaction from the
dog. A certain level of fear should be expected from a kitten that has
never been exposed to dogs before. Time and gradual exposure work
well.

I like to put the dog and cat on separate sides of a baby gate
because this allows them to get used to seeing each other with minimal
stress for both parties. Dogs with high prey and/or predatory drives
may not be suited to live peacefully with cats. Although I have known
bull terriers that lived harmoniously with cats, if you called me on the
telephone and asked me if I thought it would be a good idea for you to
get a new kitten for your adult bull terrier, my answer would be an
emphatic no. Dogs bred to hunt small game are, for obvious reasons, a
higher risk when it comes to keeping them with cats.

The truth is that cats own the house they live in. The humans
know it, the cats know it, it's just that the puppy needs to learn it. Cats
can be very good teachers too, but it depends on the temperament of
your cat. If you have the type of cat that is going to run away from
your new dog, then we have a common scenario. Dogs love to chase.
They will run down just about anything that stimulates their prey
drive. It is important to have good physical control of your puppy or
adult dog when making first-time introductions. The cat should not be
held or physically forced to confront the new dog. Time allotted for
the initial introductions should be brief. If your cat has nails, just be
careful. This arrangement works out more often than not, so give it
time. Separate them by a gate or screen door. The more they get used
to seeing each other, the better. If you have a puppy, then you will be

using a training crate, and this in itself will help your cat to get comfortable with your new pup.

When introducing your old dog to your new cat there are a couple of different strategies to consider. One way would be to crate the new cat and allow your dog to go over and investigate without being able to actually make contact with the cat. This must also be done with your dog on a leash just in case the dog is intent on terrorizing the cat. If this situation occurs, you will correct your dog for his bad behavior. When a dog is fixed intensely on a cat and shows any indication of serious aggression, then the experiment is over and you should not go any further.

I have asked clients to board their dogs out in a kennel as a way of temporarily displacing the dog and thus allowing the cat to establish its territory. While the dog is away, the cat will surely scent the existence of the dog and not be shocked at seeing him upon his arrival home. Dogs brought into the house after a week away are ready to accept a bit of a change in the old routine, so this is a good time to make first introductions. Remember to act like today is a new day, and guess what? There is a cat in the house, oh boy! and isn't he nice?

Having a well-trained dog helps this new cat situation a whole lot. If the cat is not very nervous, then you've got it easy. Have patience and you can often work this out.

Pet Birds, Ferrets, Rabbits, etc.

Dogs can live in a multiple-species environment. We know that they can because we've seen it over and over. Television programs dedicated to the world of animals frequently show the synergy among animals. I have personally owned dogs that fared well with everything from hamsters to Amazon parrots. It is most important to recognize the intentions and drives of your dog. If you don't, then be careful as you learn them. Do not leave a new fox terrier alone with a bunch of small animals while you're shopping and expect to find everybody okay when you get back. Be careful and apply a systematic approach, using gradual exposures.

Dealing with Pet Separation

When two dogs are bonded and one passes on, the remaining dog will surely go through a period of readjustment. It is important for you, who are grieving as well, to be as strong as you can for your remaining dog. It is not good for you to cry to your dog about the loss, or change the routine your dog knows as well as he knew his partner. Please do not change any more than necessary at a time like this. Spending a great deal more of your time with the one dog now can create a stronger attachment and therefore possibly produce a separation-anxiety issue. This is interesting because many times this looks as if the remaining dog is pining away for the lost dog (pet/pet), but it is actually a classic pet/partner separation crisis. I do not mean to imply that your remaining dog is insensitive to his loss. I'm confident that he is feeling as lost as you are. I am asking you to be conscious of the way you treat him during this difficult time for both of you.

Sometimes it is wise to replace the lost dog, but you must look at your dog's situation and try to figure out what would be best for both you and him. If your dog is old, then bringing in a little puppy might be a little rough for him. Adopting a middle-aged dog might be nice, but will your old guy benefit or gain pack fulfillment from the addition of another dog? Ask yourself if this new dog will be cutting your old dog out of affection or special attention. If you have the room in your heart for two or more, then by all means, go for it. I know many lovely people who successfully maintain fluctuating colonies of dogs.

Afterword

Upon finishing this project, I realized that the information I provided you with must feel a bit overwhelming. Although I tried to keep my text as basic as possible so as to communicate my message clearly, this business of dogs can be confusing. My aim here has been to teach you the great lessons that I have learned from dogs and their people. Living in this dog zone over the past twenty-five years has taught me how to direct dogs' strengths as well as weaknesses, how to be firm yet friendly, and how to recognize when to leave well enough alone. It has been an interesting education and I thank you for sharing in it. For me, living in a world without dogs would be like having sound without music. I hope that you feel the same way too after having your own dog experiences. Proceed with knowledge, as well as questions all the days that you are with dogs. Enjoy your dogs as I am certain that they will enjoy you. I welcome you to a new and wonderful world. Good luck.

Appendix I: Your Dog's General Health and Behavior

By Joseph M. Carrillo, D.V.M.,
Dip. ACVIM, and Deborah Sarfaty, D.V.M.

For the owner, keeping a dog healthy takes dedication and commitment. For the veterinarian, it means providing proper and responsible medical care. When medical problems do arise, *most are simple*. When they are not, owner compliance and possible financial burdens have to be considered.

It all seems so simple at the outset. Yet the responsibility of pet ownership has far-reaching emotional, logistical, and financial implications. This appendix is an attempt to provide you, the new pet owner, with guidelines to insure that your pet's well health care is properly provided.

Obviously, there is no way to include in these few pages all aspects of pet selection and potential medical/surgical problems. Which pets will live long and prosper (so to speak) and which ones will have problems is difficult to predict. Veterinarians, not unlike physicians, will attempt to maximize the quality and duration of your pet's life. All owners should feel comfortable with their veterinarian(s) and be able to rely on their expertise when faced with *any* medical/surgical problem(s) that may affect their pet.

The following text contains information on general health issues:

Well Health
Care Examination

Once you have selected your pet, it is wise to have it examined by a veterinarian. During the initial visit, a complete history and physical examination will be performed. Your veterinarian will examine the eyes, ears, nose, and throat. The heart and lungs will be listened to. The abdomen and lymph nodes will be palpated. The hair coat and skin health will be assessed. Your pet's gait will be observed. The muscles and bones will be manipulated for soundness. The general conformation and breed standards will also be assessed. Any obvious deformity will be noted. A recorded rectal temperature and body weight completes the exam.

The duration of your dog's first exam is variable. Depending on the physical findings and need for discussion, the usual exam lasts fifteen to twenty minutes.

Vaccination Protocol

Most puppies are sold or obtained around eight weeks of age. Consequently, your first exam may also include vaccinations. Generally, dogs are vaccinated against the canine distemper virus, parvo virus, adeno and parainfluenza virus, and leptospirosis bacterium (DA2PPL). This combined vaccine should be administered three times over an eight-week period (i.e. at eight weeks, at twelve weeks, and at fourteen to sixteen weeks). This type of schedule maximizes the potential for protective immunity against these potentially fatal diseases. By fourteen weeks of age, your dog is immunologically capable of processing any vaccine. Therefore, at fourteen to sixteen weeks of age, your dog should also be vaccinated against the rabies virus. The distemper vaccine booster is given yearly. Most rabies vaccines are formulated to provide a three-year immunity. Depending on the rabies regulations and public health recommendations in your state, this vaccine might be administered more frequently. In areas where Lyme disease is prevalent, a Lyme vaccine may also be recommended. This vaccine is given twice at three-week intervals and then boostered yearly.

It is important to booster these vaccines every year. Without protection, there is always the possibility that your dog will contract a serious viral disease. These diseases are now somewhat rare in this country but only because of the concerted effort on the part of veterinarians to maintain a constant immunization schedule. Failure to adhere to recommended schedules of vaccination can shorten your pet's life span! It is also more costly to treat the disease rather than to prevent its occurrence.

Parasites

Vascular Parasites

Heartworm is a potentially fatal disease. Some areas of the country are more endemic than others, depending upon mosquito exposure. This disease is transmitted to the dog via the bite of an infected mosquito. Yearly heartworm tests along with monthly or daily preventative medications should be included in well health care for dogs.

Intestinal Parasites

Intestinal parasites are a common problem in puppies. Owners will most often report diarrhea or bloody stools. A stool sample will easily determine if your dog's clinical signs are associated with this problem. A fecal flotation will reveal microscopic eggs laid by the adult parasite. A direct fecal smear can also be examined for parasites. Roundworm, hookworm, and whipworm eggs have specific shapes and sizes that are easily identifiable. *Giardia* is a common flagellate parasite that is easily identified when infested stool is suspended in a saline solution and viewed under a microscope. Tapeworms shed segments from the body of the adult worm. These segments tend to migrate to the area around the anus opening and can be seen with the naked eye. They resemble kernels of white rice. Because of irritation created by the moving segments, dogs are often taken to the veterinarian for excessive licking, scooting, or biting at the tail base area. A portion of the tapeworm life cycle is spent within the flea. If a flea infected with tapeworm larvae is ingested by a dog, the dog will develop tapeworm infection. The larvae will become adults within the dog's intestinal tract and begin to shed segments. Obviously, flea control along with parasite-specific drug therapy are required to eradicate the problem. Deworming is a common part of your pet's first well health care visits. These medications can be given by injection, liquid, tablets, or granules. A second deworming is usually scheduled in two to three weeks. The repeat treatment is essential because the medications destroy the adults only. It takes two to three weeks for the surviving eggs to develop into adults. There are specific preventative heartworm medications that can *also* prevent reinfestation caused by intestinal parasites including hookworms, roundworms, and whipworms.

External Parasites—Fleas

Fleas are more than just a nuisance. Without treatment, they can cause severe skin disease, tapeworm infection, anemia, and even death.

Typically, flea bites produce allergic skin reactions causing hair loss and itchiness. Because fleas are bloodsucking parasites, they can bite you and your family if there is no dog to feed upon!

As little as 10 percent of the flea's life is spent on your dog. The adult female ingests blood and lays eggs. The eggs then fall off your pet and into the surrounding environment, where they develop into larvae, pupae, and adults. These four stages of the flea life cycle may be present in your home and must be eliminated by extermination.

Extermination of fleas can only be successful with a coordinated effort between you and your veterinarian. Your dog should be flea bathed and/or dipped on the same day that you choose to exterminate. Thorough vacuuming is recommended prior to extermination to help eliminate flea feces, eggs, larvae, and pupae. Both human and pet bedding should be washed well.

Extermination can be accomplished with flea bombs or foggers. The bombs can destroy larvae and adults on contact. Consequently, owners will feel immediate relief from being bit by fleas. In severe cases, professional extermination is required. It is important to remember that you and your pet's absence from the house for two to four hours during the bombing is essential! A residual chemical house spray is then recommended to eliminate surviving fleas as well as eggs and newly hatching larvae.

Sprays, powders, foam, insecticidal shampoos, dips, and collars may be advised for ongoing flea prevention. Newer preparations, such as Frontline, Advantage, and Defend, are said to have a 90 percent

effectiveness for residual flea control. These products are applied topically and are considered to be significantly safer than many of the previously existing pesticides. Program (lufenuron) is a once-a-month
flea tablet that prevents the flea eggs from hatching. This breaks the
flea life cycle and keeps fleas from surviving in your home. It is also
available in liquid form for cats.

Dogs that are hypersensitive to the flea saliva will continue to
scratch despite flea elimination. This often causes dermatitis, which
may require treatment. Sometimes, dogs develop a condition called
hot spots. The skin becomes irritated, and the normal skin/bacterial
barrier is lost. This leads to a bacterial skin infection that is character-
ized by medium to large circular, red, raw, moist lesions. These are
typically observed in large, longhaired breeds on the face, neck, side of
the rear limbs, and rump. This complication may require thorough
clipping, cleansing, application of drying agents and corticosteroids
(cortisone) to break the itch cycle. A short course of cortisone should
not have long-lasting or permanent side effects on your dog.

A simple protocol for flea management is as follows:

1. Flea bath/dip pet.

2. Vacuum rugs, couches, floor thoroughly.

3. Flea bomb or exterminate while your pet is being treated.

4. Treat dog regularly with spray, foam, powder, collar, or monthly
medications as directed.

5. Treat the home with residual chemicals.

There is no guaranteed solution to the problem of fleas! The best
approach is a concerted effort directed against the adult fleas on your
dog and against the immature stages of fleas in your home environment.

External Parasites—Ticks

Another external parasite that is common in the dog is the tick.
Many ticks serve as carriers for infectious diseases in the United States.
Some are communicable not only to dogs but also to humans.
Examples of these infectious diseases include Rocky Mountain spotted
fever, Lyme disease, and Ehrlichiosis.

The ordinary dog tick is considered to be a three-host tick. This means that the larvae, nymphs, and adults all engorge blood from dogs. The bite of the tick causes local irritation to the dog's skin. The tick passes through three stages in its life. First the six-legged larvae feed on the dog for a few days, drop off, and molt to the eight-legged nymph. Then nymphs feed on the dog for about a week, drop off, and molt into male and female adults. Females are fertilized on the dog and feed for one to three weeks. They become greatly engorged with blood before dropping to the ground to lay their eggs several weeks later. The engorged female ticks are most noticeable when attached to the dog. Removal of the tick is relatively simple. Grasping the base of its head and pulling gently with a tweezer ususally frees the tick. It is important to remove the tick's mouth parts to avoid local inflammation and continued irritation of the skin.

In the Northeast, there is a species of tick (*Ixodes dammini*) that has a life cycle associated with the white-tailed deer. The commonly called "deer tick" is responsible for transmitting a microscopic organism (*Borrelia burgdorferi*) to both dogs and humans causing Lyme disease. In dogs, Lyme disease can cause lethargy, fever, lameness, joint swelling, and muscle stiffness. In some cases, cardiac muscle damage and kidney tissue destruction can occur with lifelong compromise of organ function. Based upon clinical signs and appropriate laboratory data, a diagnosis of Lyme disease can be made. Prompt examination and diagnosis by your veterinarian is crucial for successful treatment. The disease is treated with specific antibiotics, which are also recommended for people.

Various methods of control are indicated to prevent tick infestation. Tick collars, dips, powders, and sprays will kill ticks to some extent. If tick infestation is recurrent and severe, dipping followed by topical monthly skin applications of an insecticide can be used. Frontline™ or Topspot™ kills ticks on dogs or cats for one month or more. The ticks are killed within forty-eight hours of application. Unlike many other flea and tick products, Frontline is reported to remain effective even after bathing or swimming. Your veterinarian can help recommend the method of tick treatment(s) needed for your pet.

Common Puppy Ailments

Kennel Cough

If you have purchased your puppy from a pet store, there is a possibility that your new friend will develop a hoarse cough. Occasionally, they may vomit at the end of the cough spasm. Your dog may still seem alert and responsive during and after these attacks. What your pet is likely experiencing is infectious tracheobronchitis (kennel cough). This is a highly contagious upper respiratory condition common to dogs. Several viruses, bacteria, and mycoplasma have been determined to be involved in the etiology of kennel cough. Clinical signs are usually related to irritation at the tracheobronchial level of the respiratory tract. The most common symptom is a dry, harsh tracheal cough. The dog may frequently gag and choke in an attempt to clear the air passage. Not unlike the human cold virus, this is a self-limiting process. Typically, the signs last seven to ten days. Cough suppressants and antibiotics may be helpful. On occasion, bacterial infiltration of the air sacs can cause pneumonia. If your pet exhibits signs of labored breathing and a persistent moist cough, it is important to have your dog examined.

Preventative intranasal vaccines are available for dogs that need to be kenneled during their lifetime. These vaccines are reported to impart better immunity than injectable forms, since they stimulate local immunity to both the upper and lower airways.

Vomiting

Vomiting is another common ailment of puppies. Ususally the vomitus is of a yellow or foamy character. Sometimes the vomiting is associated with parasitism. Other times it is associated with diet. Puppy pica tendencies can lead to intermittent vomiting. Puppy pica is the condition whereby a puppy ingests indigestible material, which often results in vomiting, diarrhea, or, worse, abdominal surgery to remove the foreign material from the stomach or intestines. Viruses should also be considered as a cause for vomiting, particularly when associated with diarrhea and appetite loss. When your dog begins to vomit, *do not feed him for twenty-four hours*: offer water in small amounts equal to what your dog has been known to drink. If you have a toy breed puppy, apply Karo syrup to the gums four to five times during the fasting period. These puppies may not be able to sustain normal blood sugar levels. They are prone to transient low blood sugar, which can lead to disorientation, confusion, and seizures.

Ear Mites

Puppies are particularly susceptible to intense irritation of the external ear canal and adjacent skin caused by ear mites. A characteristic, copious, dark-colored discharge often accumulates in the ear. The puppy will scratch at the ears and shake its head, sometimes violently. In long-eared dogs, there is the potential for blood vessels to rupture in the pinna of the ear. This results in an aural hematoma, which is a variable-size fluctuant swelling of the ear flap. Ear mites are easily diagnosed by physical and microscopic examination. Treatment is usually successful with eardrops.

Demodectic Mange

Demodex canis is a tiny, wormlike mite with short, stubbly legs that lives in the hair follicles and sebaceous glands of dogs. Demodex canis is present, in small numbers, on the skin of most normal dogs. Puppies acquire Demodex canis infection from their infested mothers during the nursing period. Most cases of demodectic mange occur between three to six months of age. Affected dogs harbor much larger than normal populations of Demodex as a result of an inherited defect in the immune system, cell-mediated immunodeficiency. Circumscribed areas of redness and hair loss are seen about the eyes, mouth, and bony projections on the extremities. Pruritus or itchiness is not common. If the condition is local (one or two lesions only), topical therapy is usually successful. The majority of mild cases spontaneously resolve within four to eight weeks. In generalized demodicosis, the hair becomes sparse over wider expanses and the skin becomes coarse, dry, and erythematous ("red mange"). Sometimes pustules develop, break open, ooze, and create an associated disagreeable odor. Generalized demodicosis is difficult to treat. Patience, care, and close cooperation between the pet owner and veterinarian are necessary for successful treatment. The hair on the entire dog should be clipped and kept short during treatment. Only two topical products (a ronnel-propylene glycol mixture and amitraz) are accepted as effective treatments for generalized demodicosis. The drug ivermectin, which comes from a family of chemically altered fermentation products, is currently used as a systemic therapy. The shar-pei and other loose-skinned breeds of dog are more susceptible to the generalized form.

Sarcoptic Mange

Sarcoptes scabiei causes sarcoptic mange or scabies in man, dogs, and other domestic animals. Although sarcoptic mange is relatively species specific (that is, man to man, dog to dog, pig to pig, etc.), interspecies transmission does occur, resulting in a dermatitis that is atypical and transient. There is a relatively high rate of transmission of the canine scabies mite to those people who have close contact with an infected dog. In people, the mite invades the epidermis, causing an itchy rash on the forearm, chest, abdomen, and thighs.

Sarcoptic mange of domestic animals usually starts on relatively hairless areas of the skin but may later generalize if undiagnosed or untreated. In dogs, the elbow, hock, ventral thorax, and margin of the ear pinna are typical starting places. Early lesions consist of redness, circular scabs, and pimple-like lesions. Due to intense pruritus, the scratching and rubbing by the animal causes excoriations and crusts of dried blood and serum. As the disease intensifies the skin thickens, dries, and wrinkles. Secondary bacterial infections, as seen with demodicosis, is also common.

There are several acceptable methods of treatment. Treatment consists of clipping the patient's hair and cleansing the skin with a keratolytic and antiseborrheic shampoo, and treating with a miticide. Various topically applied scabicides include ronnel, lindane, rotenone, and amitraz. Ivermectin is currently used as a systemic form of therapy.

Malformations and Disease Predisposition

Open Fontanel

Failure of the skull bone plates to fuse over the top of the head results in a defect called "open fontanel." This anomaly by itself is not associated with clinical signs. However, when examination of the puppy reveals an enlarged, domed-shaped cranium along with open fontanels, a related condition known as hydrocephalus should be considered. Here, an alteration in the normal production, flow, and absorption of cerebrospinal fluid causes cerebrocortical brain tissue destruction. Clinical signs include continual vocalizing (barking/whining), visual and auditory impairment, altered mental status, and an abnormal gait. Epizootiological studies of canine hydrocephalus reveal that brachycephalic (pug, bulldog, Lhasa Apso, Shih Tzu) and miniature breeds (e.g., Chihuahua, Yorkshire terrier, English bulldog, Maltese, Lhasa Apso, and toy poodle) are at higher risk. Some types of hydrocephalus can be managed medically and/or surgically. A veterinary neurologist can assist you in determining what course of management to pursue.

Snorting and Snoring

Upper respiratory signs are common in brachycephalic breeds. Brachycephalic refers to the conformation of the face (short snout, flat face, and stout neck). The compactness of the facial and neck region predisposes these breeds to difficulty in exchanging air in a normal manner. Consequently, they tend to snort and snore more than other breeds.

Poodles and Yorkshire terriers are prone to having collapsing tracheas. When this happens, the windpipe weakens and collapses on itself, causing abnormal airflow during inhaling and exhaling. Affected dogs have a characteristic "honking" type of cough. Prolonged and persistent symptoms may lead to pulmonary resistance and stress on the right side of the heart muscle. Most cases of collapsing trachea do not require extensive medical management. Because of respiratory limitations, these dogs are more prone to heat intolerance and should not be overly exercised for prolonged periods of time. When circumstances dictate, your veterinarian can help outline a diagnostic and therapeutic plan consistent with your dog's needs.

Outer Ear Infection

Long-eared dogs have more of a tendency to develop outer-ear infections, particularly in warm weather. Your pet may show symptoms of such an infection by starting to rub, scratch, or shake its head.

Often owners may notice varying degrees of ear discharge (wax or pus) and odor. If a dog is vigorously scratching at his ears, a small blood vessel can rupture within the ear pinna. This causes the ear flap to become distended, resulting in an aural hematoma. The ear flap will appear swollen but not painful. This condition usually requires surgical correction. Uncomplicated ear infections can be treated with topical medications. More serious conditions may require ear canal irrigation, antibiotics, and corticosteroids. In young puppies ear mites may be the inciting cause of the local irritation and subsequent inflammation. Cleansing of the ear canal and appropriate ear medications usually resolve the problem easily.

Balance problems can result from untreated ear infections. The infection can extend from the middle-ear cavity into the inner-ear cavity. The inner-ear structures detect precise head position relative to the body and coordinate with the brain to provide balance. If a balance disorder occurs, your pet may act disoriented and uncoordinated. A head tilt and spontaneous "jerky" eyeball movements may be noticed. Vomiting may occur from nausea.

Congenital Deafness

Nerve deafness is a result of an abnormality of the receptor organ within the inner ear or the peripheral hearing pathway. Congenital deafness in dogs is usually associated with hypoplasia or aplasia of the spiral organ, which means their auditory tissue may have developed only partially or not at all. A hereditary predisposition for this condition has been suggested for Old English sheepdogs, cocker spaniels, Dalmatians, and bull terriers. Neonatal and young immature dogs typically have hearing deficits detected soon after birth. But a definitive diagnosis of deafness is made by testing brain stem auditory-evoked responses. A veterinary neurologist can assist you with further information.

Appendix II: You Are What You Eat: Canine Nutrition

By Jane Bicks, D.V.M.

You are what you eat, and the same goes for your dog. While it's easy to realize how basic food, treats, and other supplements are going to contribute to your dog's general body growth and condition, his behavior and training capabilities are also affected. While every dog is different and requires his own food and supplement program, there are certain rules for good nutritional care that all owners need to follow in order for their dogs to live long healthy and happy lives. Once the basics are understood, food selection, feeding programs, and supplements can be tailored for your dog.

Nutritional Rules for Puppies

A puppy can be defined as a dog over four to six weeks of age, but under one year. If you are feeding your new dog a supermarket-bought major brand food, it must be for puppies. Canned or dry is acceptable but be aware that semimoist foods often contain dyes and sugars and can affect your puppy's behavior.

If you purchase a high-quality major brand food from your veterinarian or pet supply store, you can buy either adult or puppy food. The higher quality adult foods have enough good quality protein, fat, calcium, phosphorous, and other minerals and vitamins to support the growth of any puppy. The puppy foods generally differ by containing more calories and smaller dry food pieces. If you only have one dog and it happens to be a puppy that doesn't have a weight problem, then you will find that the puppy food allows you to put less food in the dish than food that is made for an adult dog. If your puppy is a small breed, he may be more comfortable with the smaller size dry nugget, yet many small breeds will prefer adult-size nuggets.

Puppies need to eat throughout the day so they have the nutrients required as the various portions of their bodies demand them. The three popular puppy-feeding programs are: free feeding, portion-controlled feeding, and meal feeding.

Free Feeding

All you have to do is put a lot of food into a dish and allow your puppy to nibble throughout the day. While it is the easiest way to feed a puppy, it is not my favorite. This method will not work with canned food because it has the potential to spoil and attract insects. It also doesn't work for the owner who is responsible enough to want to know how much their puppy is eating day by day (appetites vary as puppies grow), and if they are in fact eating. One of the first signs of illness in a puppy is lack of appetite.

Portion-Controlled Feeding

This is probably one of the most popular feeding methods. After placing the manufacturer's recommended amount of food (adjusting to your puppy's growing weight) into your puppy's dish once during the day, your puppy is allowed to nibble throughout. While some puppies will eat a day's supply at one sitting, most will portion control their appetite, eating as their body requires the nutrients. Studies have demonstrated that if puppies are brought up with this type of feeding program, they will not overeat as food portion-controlled adults, while adults not used to having food left out all day are almost certain to eat the food within a short amount of time. But if you are having problems housebreaking your puppy, this food regimen is probably not for you.

Meal Feeding

This technique is most common with canned food, at-home moms, or for puppies that are being housebroken. With this method, food is fed at certain intervals during the day. I prefer three meals divided throughout the twenty-four hours (as equal as possible, without losing a night's sleep). Two meals daily can start at about age five to six months. Once-a-day feeding is not acceptable for any age or type dog.

Supplementing your puppy's food with table scraps and most types of vitamin/mineral products is not recommended. Introducing table scraps into your puppy's food will create a finicky eater, while the addition of separate minerals or vitamins can be very dangerous and/or useless. Additional calcium does not help bone growth or self-standing ears but can cause bone problems. The addition of multinutritional supplements can be as dangerous as single ones, since they can unbalance the carefully balanced food you've selected to feed your dog.

A supermarket food can generally be supplemented with any type of multivitamin, mineral, amino acid, fatty acid product without destroying the balance. There are many good one-a-day-type supplements available if you just want to make sure your puppy is getting everything he needs. If your puppy's skin or coat is dry, there are supplements formulated specifically for skin and coat. Omega-3 oils are the newest skin and coat supplements. Combined with other oils and support nutrients, they can work wonders.

My choice of a well-rounded one-a-day-type supplement, especially for the better quality foods, are whole natural foods, which include brewer's yeast, spirulina, barley or wheat grass, and bee pollen. These contain multiple nutrients that are balanced by nature and don't interfere with any type of food.

A puppy's weight must be noted every week. You will adjust his food intake depending upon your evaluation. A fat puppy may be cute but can develop bone disease. A large-breed puppy should not blossom and become the he-man you want until he is at least two years old. The best way to determine if your puppy is fat or thin is by feeling for his ribs. Place your puppy between your legs, or on the table, with the head facing forward. Putting one hand on the left shoulder, the other on the right shoulder, press and move backward over the ribs toward the tail. If your puppy is at his correct weight, you will feel his ribs with just a pinch of fat and muscle under your hands. More than a pinch of fat indicates that he is too fat, while feeling every rib in detail (unless a greyhound, whippet-type dog) means he's too thin.

People food should only be given as an additional meal or in place of a treat. If you are so convinced that your puppy needs calcium, put some cottage cheese or scrambled eggs into his dish. Generally, puppies do not have a problem with milk, while older dogs can develop lactose intolerence (just like us), causing diarrhea. You can save your chicken, fish, or beef leftovers to use as food rewards, but the bones are not allowed.

Make sure that your puppy's feeding place is set up correctly. A weighted water dish and a separate food dish should be placed away from the normal household traffic. Competitive eating with family members or other dogs can cause your puppy to eat too fast and immediately regurgitate. Since plastic dishes can cause allergy in dogs, I prefer stainless steel or ceramic ones. Whether you place the dishes on the floor or on a food stand will depend on the type of puppy you have. Large-breed puppies will need to have their dishes raised as they grow. One of the most common causes of bloat is the bending down of a dog to eat its food. Bloat is a condition where there is a sudden distension of the stomach with food, gas, and gastric secretions. This is a life-threatening condition that requires immediate medical attention.

Treat selection is very important at this young age. I prefer pieces of carrots, celery, and apples, especially since most dog and puppy foods don't contain that type of healthy fiber for intestinal and oral health. Freeze-dried liver or chicken treats are alternatives, but keep in mind that liver can cause diarrhea. Leftover chicken, beef, or fish is another choice of healthy treats. No foods or treats with sugars, dyes, or preservatives should be used.

Puppy Problems and Nutritional Solutions

Excessive Chewing and Biting

- Try using natural hard chews such as hooves, ears, and rawhide.
- Give him real beef bones once a week only.
- Try different types of dry foods—oftentimes the larger and harder the better.
- Put the food into a toy called the Buster Cube™. This toy

releases dry food as the dog pushes it around, thus the dog uses up energy while being reinforced for using the cube.

Problems with Housebreaking

- Do not entirely withhold water.

- Feed two to three times daily along with a toilet schedule.

- Feed a high-quality pet food with a digestibility of at least 90 percent. The higher the digestibility the less feces. Call or write the manufacturer for the information.

- If the stool is loose and has been checked by your veterinarian, add brewer's yeast and bran to the food. Start with one-eighth teaspoon for small puppies, one-quarter teaspoon for medium, one-half teaspoon for large. Increase slowly over one to two weeks until the stool gets firmer.

Fear and Anxiety

Sometimes a dog can be anxious or fearful for no apparent reason. These symptoms can also prevent a dog from settling down at night and thereby can keep both you and your dog from getting a good night's sleep. If so, try the following:

- Try portion-control feeding in a quiet place so the dog can nibble all day.

- Select a food that contains wheat. The by-products of wheat digestion can act on the centers of the brain that calm.

- Add kava kava to the water. This herb can be bought in liquid form manufactured for children, but if using a dry herb, it can be mixed in the food. Dosage: large-breed puppy—one-half of the human dosage twice daily. Small-breed puppy—one-sixth of the human dosage twice daily.

- Try giving warm milk plus honey and a dog biscuit. This will activate the calming center of the brain.

- Try giving Bach's Rescue Remedy, which is available in health food stores. Buy the liquid form, without alcohol, and add it to the dog's water or place directly into the mouth. Dosage is the same as kava kava. Can be used with kava kava or the warm milk and honey.

- Try giving Calms, manufactured by Hyland's, which is available in health food stores. One tablet for small-breed puppies, two tablets for medium- and large-breed puppies. Use as often as every four to six hours. Place in food or directly into the mouth. It is a combination of homeopathic ingredients.

Pica

This condition occurs when your puppy keeps trying to eat things that he shouldn't. If this occurs, try the following:

- If feeding a supermarket food, change to a better quality or add a supplement.
- If feeding a high-quality food, add a "whole food" supplement.
- Add tomato juice to the food to deter stool eating.
- Change the puppy's food, depending on what he is chewing on. Try to "match" the mouth feel. If you are feeding canned food and your puppy is eating rocks, let's change to dry food.

Fatigue and Poor Attention Span

If your puppy tires easily or has a poor attention span, but the veterinary health checkup is okay, then try the following:

- Assuming your puppy is over six weeks old, only feed twice a day.
- Feed a high-quality protein food with no more than two cereals in the first seven ingredients.
- Make sure your puppy's food has a total digestibility of at least 90 percent.
- Add an omega-3 fatty acid supplement to the food or as a healthy treat. These oils include flaxseed, borage, and fish oil. Combined with regular oils such as corn (omega-6), they are known to increase concentration—and a shiny coat.
- Brewer's or torula yeast is full of protein plus B vitamins and

is a great supplement. Follow recommended dosage. Bee pollen and propolis—follow directions for humans and adjust.

Difficulty Learning to Sit or to Come

- Feel for your puppy's ribs. If he's too fat, chances are he is growing too fast and his bones ache. Feed less food. If feeding puppy food, change to an adult food. If your veterinarian does diagnose panosteitis (growing pains), arnica is the remedy of choice. Dosages for large-breed puppies are the same as for an adult dog. For medium-breed puppy, one-half of the adult dosage. For a small-breed puppy, one-quarter of the adult dose.

Nervous, High-strung

- Keep the puppy's tummy full. Feed portion control. Use the Buster Cube toy.

- Use food that contains wheat in the first four ingredients.

- Use food that does not contain high quantities of meat protein (22 percent or below).

- Use food that contains at least two to three cereals in the first seven ingredients.

- Add brewer's yeast (B vitamins) to the food or use it as a treat.

- Try giving Calms pills. (See "Fear and Anxiety" above for dosage.)

- Give no food or treats with dyes, preservatives, or sugars of any types. Note that sucrose and fructose are sugars. Malt is often sweetened with sugar. Molasses is also sugar.

Nutritional Rules for Adult Dogs

Use the same puppy rules above, changing the course to adult food. If your dog is not used to being fed free food, don't do it unless you want a blimp. If your older dog has lost a significant number of teeth, canned food is best for him.

If your dog is overweight, a diet is mandatory and not as difficult as you would think:

- Feed 25 percent less than the recommended amount of nondiet food throughout the day. The more times your dog eats, the more calories he will burn. For example, if your dog should be fed four cups of food daily, feed three-quarters of a cup, four times a day. Weigh your dog and mark the weight on a chart along with the estimated amount of fat over his ribs.

- The only treats allowed are cooked or fresh vegetables and popcorn.

- An exercise program must be initiated, starting slowly but followed every day.

- If your dog has not lost one to two pounds per month (fast weight loss will result in immediate weight gain), then you have to change to a diet food. That food should also be fed as often as possible and used along with an exercise program.

Aging dogs are similar to aging people. Prevention will help a dog live a longer, healthier, and happier life. Antioxidants are a must, starting from two years of age. Antioxidants can include vitamins C, E, and beta-carotene. There are many antioxidant canine formulas available, and many of them are in treat form. Adding green "whole foods," such as broccoli, is an excellent source of antioxidants and additional nutrients. Omega-3 oils are essential to help relieve the aches and pains your older dog will eventually develop. They will also increase his mental acuity. These are available in treat form.

If you don't have an exercise program for your dog, develop one now. Start slowly, but gradually build it up.

Adult Dog Problems and Nutritional Solutions

Excessive Chewing and Biting
See puppy solution.

Pica
See puppy solution.

Fear and/or Anxiety
See puppy solutions. Or try giving your dog valerian, in capsule or liquid form (without alcohol). Dosage: large-breed dog, same as adult, every four hours; medium-breed dog, one-half adult dosage; small-breed dog, one-quarter of the adult dosage.

Begging (Always Hungry)
- Change to a food with higher fiber to help "fill" the dog.

- Change to a better quality food that will satisfy your dog's requirements for nutrients.

- Give treats that are really supplements. For example, give a multiple vitamin/mineral wafer.

- Use the "Buster Cube" toy.

- Try the *Garcinia cambogia* herb, which is also known as citramax. Many diet products combine this herb with stimulants. Do not use these; use only *pure* citramax or Garcinia cambogia. Dosage: large-breed dogs, human dosage one hour prior to a meal or in the meal; medium-breed dogs, one-half of the human dosage; small-breed dogs, one-quarter of the human dosage.

From just these few pages, it's easy to see that your dog really is the result of his diet and that changes in diet and the addition of supplements can modify any dog's behavior. If you are still not convinced let me share a story with you. A New York City dog was having a problem—his owner would come home and find him drunk every night. Thinking that the dog had a medical problem, the owner called me to control the drinking problem. When I arrived at the house, not only did I find a drunk dog, but also the furniture was destroyed and the carpet torn. The dog was medically sound, except that he was four sheets to the wind. The problem was both behavioral and nutritional. You see, the dog was a high-strung breed living in an apartment alone from 7 A.M. until 8 P.M. To make matters worse, he was being fed a semimoist food, loaded with dyes and sugars. Once the sugar high ended early in the morning, the dog became hungry and angry, wanting more sugar. The destruction was the result of boredom and anger, while the drunkenness was because the dog was smart enough to know that the liquor bottles contained sugar. No matter where the owner placed the bottles, the dog had all day to find them and get drunk. Between changing the food to a high-fiber dry food fed portion controlled, adding valerian to the drinking water, enacting behavior modification, and leaving the liquor out of the house for a few months, the dog was back to being a sober nondestructive dog. It's remarkable what nutrition can do.

Acknowledgments

I have always been lucky. I have a great family, great friends, and have always had great dogs. I grew up in a modest apartment building in the Bronx, sharing a two-bedroom apartment with my mother and father, four siblings, two German shepherds, and a Russian blue cat. We always were and continue to be a close family. I must say, though, that my parents stood divided on the dog issue, with my dad feeling that dogs should be on farms, while my mom just kept bringing them home. So, Mom, thanks for being so dog oriented. Luckily, I married Sabine Majowski, who also loves animals. Our two children, Jessica and Gavin, are genetically predisposed and just as dog crazy too.

There is a T-shirt sold for dog trainers that reads: "The only thing two dog trainers can agree on is that what the third one is doing is wrong." Sorry, some dog trainers are still in the habit of spreading gossip and innuendo about their peers. There are, however, many people "in the business" whom I respect and admire, and although many of them do not get along well with one another, I love them all. Captain Arthur Haggerty, if a little information fell out of your head, I hope that I was there to catch it. Carol Benjamin, I am grateful to you for being my friend. Loren Manzel, thanks for your insight into the canine mind and body. Sue Sternberg, I know for sure that we will someday be old dog people together, thanks for everything. Larry Berg is still the only private dog trainer I know who does not work on the weekends—you are amazing. I lost two friends in the past couple of years who had greatly influenced my way of thinking on dogs—Job Michael Evans and Ruth Sundeen. I remember your love for dogs and I miss you guys.

The sport friends who I have gained over the years truly enlightened me to an exciting area of dog training. Thank you Ed Frawley for introducing me to Gisela Engel who imported "Fred Arabela CS" to me. This dog was all you said that he was, truly a dog with magnificent character, thank you both. I want to thank Gisela for introducing me to Michael and Linda Zenobia. Gisela, you were right, Mike is magical with his "reads" on drives and consequent training reinforcement. Mike and Linda, I appreciate your putting up with all my questions for all these years. I hope I get an opportunity to train in your Schutzhund club in the not-too-distant future.

The veterinary field has been kind to me as well. The study of veterinary technology has risen up from the ground and is clearly headed for the sky. I owe most of my professional success to Dr. Jack Burke and his family. The Burkes basically took my hand and walked me through the veterinary technology field. They offered me the opportunity to work with veterinary and behavioral specialists for many years prior to my branching out on my own. My teaching position at Mercy College was granted by Dr. Burke based on my veterinary technology license. Dr. Joseph Carrillo is board certified in internal medicine. When Joe and I worked together, his interest was neurology. I was fortunate to have worked with Dr. Carrillo for a few years, and I am grateful for all that I learned by following him around. I have the greatest respect for his medical expertise. Thank you, Joe, for writing Appendix I, on health. It's super. A big thanks to Debbie Sarfaty, who co-authored the appendix on health along with Joe. Thanks Debbie for keeping Joe on target and for all your great advice. Dr. Jane Bicks is an accomplished author of several books on pet nutrition and a longtime friend. Jane, how can I thank you for taking time to write Appendix II, on nutrition, for me? Thank you for giving me your time and knowledge, you are the best. I am also grateful to the veterinary community for their support over the years.

Thanks also to my staff trainers at the Center for Animal Behavior and Canine Training, Wes Artope, Jim Boggio, and Gary Pietropaolo. I could not have done this without you guys keeping the ship afloat. With all my heart, thanks to Marie Smith, Serena Timpano, Deirdre Douglas, and Sabrina Sordo for everything you have done to help "the Center" grow—the walls would have fallen in if not for you. Chang Hyn Seo, you and your family have become dear friends. You are "gifted" in many ways, and I am sincerely thankful to you for sharing your gifts with me. Fran Daniele, I am glad you chose to do your school internship at "the Center"; you were a pleasure to have, and you did an excellent job proofreading my work. Roy Spitalnik, hang in there and do what you are doing, they call it dog training. Roy, thanks for taking good care of the "in-kennel dogs." Damien Multary, I can't wait until you graduate college, you are an animal guy and I know you will do well. Many thinks to "Hollie" Edwards, my golden retriever "demo dog," and to her folks for letting me train her. Last but not least, the Center's cats, "Shake" and "Bake," thanks for the distractions.

Noah Lukeman, literary agent and all-around good guy, you are amazing at your job. I would not be here if not for your influence. Noah, I think I can see a Fifth Avenue address in your future. Thanks for your drive. David Cashion and Hyperion, thanks for believing in me.

My clients over the years have been wonderful. All those years of house calls with so many gracious people and their dogs, I thank you. The dogs in my life, those that I have owned and those that I have known, I am indebted to you for the education that you provided me.

If I am leaving anyone out, it is a weakness of my head, not my heart.

—Steve Diller

Index